MOOD MANAGEMENT

MAKE GOOD FEELINGS LINGER
AND
BAD FEELINGS FADE

THOMAS MARRA, PHD

Archway Publishing books may be ordered through booksellers or by contacting:

Archway Publishing
1663 Liberty Drive
Bloomington, IN 47403
www.archwaypublishing.com
844-669-3957

ISBN: 978-1-4808-9393-1 (sc)

Library of Congress Control Number: 2020914707

Print information available on the last page.

Archway Publishing rev. date: 12/01/2020

Contents

List of Figures

List of Tables

About The Author

Thomas Marra received his Ph.D. from the California School of Professional Psychology (now Alliant International University) in 1981. He received a California State Scholarship to attend the University of the Pacific, then a California Fellowship to obtain his graduate degree at CSPP-San Diego. He entered the US Army in 1980 and completed his post-doctoral residency at Walter Reed Medical Center in Washington, DC. He was the 17th Infantry Division Psychologist in Monterey, California before going in private practice there, where he practiced for 35 years. He was active in outpatient, inpatient, and partial hospitalization programs. He was the founder and Clinical Director of the Monterey Psychiatric Health Facility, which received Joint Commission on the Accreditation of Healthcare Organizations with Commendation (only 2% of hospitals receive commendation status, let alone in their first year of operation). The inpatient facility was one of few in the United States owned and operated by psychologists. He received many awards for his advocacy in psychology by the California Psychological Association, where he was Chair of Committees, member of the Board of Directors, and on the Executive Committee of the Board. He is a Fellow of the American Psychological Association and Life Long Member. He is the author of *Depressed & Anxious* and *DBT in Private Practice*. He was on the Board of Directors of the Oklahoma Psychological Association. Dr. Marra has lectured widely in the US, and has presented internationally. He is currently working on social media to highlight how people can manage moods and regulate emotions, to reach an even larger audience.

Acknowledgments

I wish to thank my early professors. Ken Beauchamp, Ph.D. taught me tolerance for ambiguity. Martin Gipson, Ph.D. tolerated my incessant chatter, my frequent visits to his office just to express my enthusiasm for what I was learning, and befriended me as a colleague even though I was an undergraduate. To Julian Meltzoff, Ph.D., who in my graduate studies at CSPP-San Diego, reinforced my scientific way of thinking and chided me about my arrogance. He tried to teach me humility. May they all rest in peace. Lastly, to my mother, Iwana Minchew Marra, who tolerated and supported me from childhood to adulthood. Her most condemning remark would be "oh, you." She was quite loving. That security in the emotional bond leads to independence.

INTRODUCTION

I t is said there are three people who changed how you see the world and its contents: Copernicus (Kuhn, 1957) proved we were not the center of our solar system, Einstein (Isaacson, 2008) proved even objects all around us are not the solids we believed them to be, and to top it off Freud (1920) told us we are not even aware of the feelings we thought we had. What's up with that? If you are not the center of all things, and your world is not what the human eye beholds, and maybe you can't trust your own emotions, then what is an intelligent person to do? Turn to FOX news, CNN, or PBS to tell you what is really true? Or how about playing ostrich and just putting your head in the sand, pretending everything is okay and you just wait until everything threatening passes?

None of these things are satisfying. Why were some imprisoned or beheaded for heresy for writing that the Earth is not the center of the solar system? Plotoemy (Hoskin, 1999) attempted to explain the mathematical improbabilities of observations from common belief of the solar system by making correction after mathematical correction. He did not want to challenge the accepted assumption about the Earth as center of the solar system. And Freud spun theory after theory, few of which were ever empirically tested.

So perhaps like Copernicus you need to look at the world through fresh eyes. Unlike Ptolemy you need to stop applying old ways of doing things and expecting a different result. Like Freud and Einstein you need to look deeper into the murky waters of the self that is the subject of this book.

WHO NEEDS THIS BOOK? AND DSM

This workbook is especially relevant to simple distress; you don't have any disorder at all, you are simply less than happy with your life. If you feel that bad times outnumber good times, that bad times last longer than the good times, that much effort is required to get through the day (even though you do get through all days), and you wish to improve your emotional life – then this book is for you.

I'm not a big fan of DSM (the Diagnostic and Statistical Manual of Mental Disorders), promulgated by the American Psychiatric Association (ApA). Why do we have such a nomenclature (naming) of symptoms. For some good, practical, and bad reasons.

The good reasons are that being able to name a disorder, identify it, and differentiate it from other conditions offers specificity in research, testing, and treatment. That is all great news. And it has taken enormous resources to do it to profitable ends. We can now differentiate disorders that are primarily genetic (like the schizophrenias, which require medical-chemical solutions) from environmentally-based conditions (like common distress, adjustment disorders, most sleep disorders, most sexual disorders, and most paraphilia's) that require psychological interventions.

The "miracle of modern medicine" is not just a slogan, but in many cases a reality. I'll give a personal example. Someone in my family was diagnosed with paranoid schizophrenia during the Korean War. He was discharged from the military and given a lifetime monthly disability payment. Schizophrenia is a horrible condition, both for the person who has it as well as the family and society who are subject to it. By definition the schizophrenic does not recognize reality, if they think it is true then for them it is true. Presented with abundant evidence that their beliefs are incorrect, they cling to their beliefs. Evidence to the contrary is irrelevant, dismissed, resented, and actually fuels their convictions that they are right; it is the world that is wrong, not them. There is abundant and irrefutable evidence that schizophrenia is a genetic disorder, and only with medications can the person improve. In fact, with medications a schizophrenic can lead a "normal" life. But even with schizophrenia there is a psychological component: compliance. They frequently don't want to take their meds, and don't take them.

So naming (in this case the DSM) has a reasonable and good outcome. Now for the practical reasons. Imagine the following scenario (which is not atypical, I can tell you from my 40 years in clinical practice.)

Psychologist:	The patient was unhappy and dissatisfied with life. I therefore administered 24 sessions of psychotherapy, over a 24 week period, with between session homework assignments,
Insurance Agent:	We won't pay for it.
Psychologist:	Why?
Insurance Agent:	We don't pay for unhappy and dissatisfied.
Psychologist:	Why?
Insurance Agent:	Because "unhappy and dissatisfied" is not a medical disorder we cover.
Psychologist:	But the patient had Dysthymic Disorder, Single Episode
Insurance Agent:	Well, that is not what is in your notes, and we will not pay.

So insurance reimbursement forces us to use DSM.

Now for the bad reasons, and this has nothing to do with insurance reimbursement. Most patients present for treatment of a complex set of disorders. They don't come to the professional saying "Hello I'm Joe, and I'm coming in for treatment of my DSM 296.23." Instead they say, "Hello…I'm Joe. And…I feel really, really sad… I've never felt this way before…I mean…I don't think I'm nuts…I just can't function. There is something wrong. And I doubt myself. I'm shaky. I'm nervous. I've lost confidence. My marriage is falling apart… My kid's hate me… My penis doesn't work anymore… I'm a wreck."

We call it comorbidity. Comorbidity is when not just one thing is wrong, several things are wrong. Comorbidity used to be seen as a nuisance by researchers. For example, "Seventy-five percent of our potential subject population for our study on depression had to be eliminated because they met the criteria for both depression disorder and an anxiety disorder." Until someone with insight said, "Hey, this is not an anomaly, this is the norm." Think about it. If you get depressed long enough, you will begin to feel anxiety that maybe the depression will never go away. Or the reverse, if you have anxiety long enough you become depressed about that. Depression and anxiety, unfortunately, go hand in hand.

So rather than throw the proverbial baby out with the bathwater, both practitioners (Marra, 2005) and researchers (Dolorosa & Pinni, 2012) began to explore the world of comorbidity.

Not surprisingly, it was attorneys who first answered the call. Yes, they would say, Jane was under the care of a psychologist and psychiatrist for the treatment of her depression prior to the accident. But when Mr. Bill T-boned her car and she lost a leg it aggravated her precondition of depression. She lost function. She had more reasons, on a daily basis, to be depressed.

If you have a depressive disorder (Major Depressive Disorder or Dysthymic Disorder), a Bipolar Disorder, an Anxiety Disorder (Panic, Social Phobia, Obsessive-Compulsive Disorder), or Impulse Control Disorder, most likely you have many (comorbid) conditions going on at the same time. The strategies in this book are robust, and are designed not to focus on just one or two disorders, but on many. No matter what the label (diagnosis), mental health issues share some commonalities: emotional pain resulting in life limitations. These limitations may be modest (as in distress) or major (as in clinical depression).

There have been many books written on thoughts and feelings, and the interplay between the two, many of which are excellent (Burns, 1980; McKay et al., 2007, 2011). This book draws from such literature and by exploring context and self we will be in a better position to wisely navigate our life.

What is context? Humans live in a world influenced by culture, family, society, and habit. Anthropologists have said humans are among the only species who self-destruct (commit suicide). Why? Because we are self-conscious. We look at ourselves and if we do not like what we see we become despondent. Maybe you look at yourself and feel pride. No other species, as far as we know, engages in this kind of self-reflection.

What is self? Your identity, how you portray yourself to yourself, is your self. This is very complicated. If you wish to portray yourself as a basically good person, but are aware of the many instances you behaved poorly, then you attempt to wear a mask or facade so others see you as you wish to be seen. You can see the interrelationship of context and self. They are two different facets of the same thing. The complexity of this issue increases when you consider the different roles you perform in your life (you want to be seen one way by your spouse, another way by your children, another way by your boss, another way by your neighbor, and yet another way by your extended family.) So the multifaceted natures of self and context make a "workbook" (or any book of any utility) problematic when you are dealing with complex issues of context. The goal is to rise above where you are to get to where you want to be.

This book is about the path of wisdom, selecting a strategy that is right for you given your context, your desired sense of self, and your willingness to do the effortful tasks of self-exploration required for change.

WHAT YOU CAN EXPECT TO GET OUT OF THIS BOOK

If you read this book, like you might a novel, you can expect to get very little out of it. Why? It is a workbook, a roadmap of sorts. And like all maps it is useless if you don't use it to make the correct turns, to avoid dead ends, and perhaps most importantly to fully understand that the destination you have plotted is really where you want to go. Instead, if you *work the book*, do all the various exercises (even when you think to yourself, "Oh, I don't need to do this one, I already know the answers."), then you are fully prepared to go to the next step.

By *working the book you can expect to:*

- more vividly experience and observe the world through increasing mindfulness
- observe more (take in more information) than previously
- have a better understanding of your emotions (why they happen)
- help positive feelings linger
- have unwanted feelings fade
- have increased confidence that you are taking the right steps toward progress
- have increased personal tool sets to make fewer repetitions of strategies that have not worked in the past for you

- understand the reciprocal relationship between you and others
- have a better understanding of how you are shaped by the environment
- have a better understanding of how you can shape your own environment
- have increased clarity about your true goals in life, for now (they may change)
- make better decisions
- have better relationships
- increase meaning in your life and have a value-based life
- have more strategies than just effort or will power
- ruminate less and have thoughts be more productive

These are tall goals. Research has shown (Minden, 2017) that having a rationale, as well as explicit instructions, increases your willingness to follow through. Therefore, before each exercise or task in this workbook you will be told:

- **What** To Do
- **Why** To Do It
- **How** To Do It

The only exception to this framework is chapter 2, which reviews what scholars write about the field of emotion regulation, where instead you will be given *The Takeaway*, or what and why the information may be relevant to you.

IMPROVE YOUR DECISION-MAKING SKILLS USING STRATEGY

This book is about how to manage or regulate your emotions better. Intertwined with that is having new tools, or old tools you fail to use, to accomplish your emotional objectives. You use strategy, or decision making, during this process. Here is a simple flow chart of the decision making process.

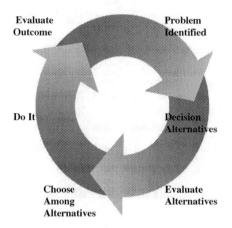

Figure 1: General Problem Solving

Now let's look at a preview of the decision-making process specifically for emotion regulation you will learn in this workbook.

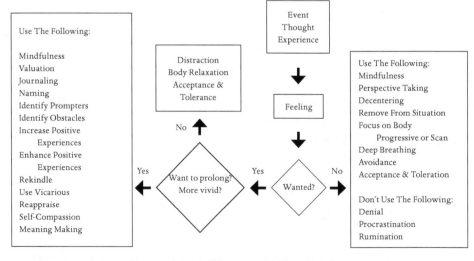

Figure 2 Emotional Problem Solving

HOW TO USE THIS BOOK

There are two temptations, different for different people, that I want you to avoid: Some want only to read the text and not do the exercises, and others want to skip the text and just do the exercises. Resist both of these temptations. The book has a flow. I invite you to follow that flow. Perhaps you have already read many other books on mindfulness, so you want to skip Chapter 3. There are many excellent books and texts on mindfulness, and perhaps you have not only read them, but gone to workshops and seminars teaching you how to do it. Great. But mindfulness is not like a task (sweeping the floor and then it is done). It must become a way of being in the world. It is never "over." To do it for a time and discard it as "done" does violence against its entire purpose. The goal is to live mindfully. Each chapter explores a different element of what it means to be fully human. Take chapter 4, "Feelings," don't say to yourself you already know your feelings, and a book (no matter how good it may be) can tell you anything you don't already know. Because you would be right on one level, nobody knows you better than you do. This chapter can make you know yourself even better. You are more complicated than you may think.

Finally, please do not jump to the Appendix and identify a symptom and go to the pages that suggest a resolution. It is intended as a prompt for those who have already worked the book and continue to struggle with issues.

The only exception to this is chapter 2. It is the scholarly review of the emotion regulation literature. If you are uninterested in the scholarship behind the recommendations and exercises in this workbook, then I would recommend that you at least look at the indented "Takeaways" listed in the chapter.

THE ROLE OF A THERAPIST OR A LIFE COACH

No book is a substitute for needed psychotherapy. And I think most clinical psychologists, psychiatrists, counselors, and life coaches will be thrilled if you brought in this book *while* you have begun your self journey. Why do most organized sports have cheerleaders? Why do many athletes find a home game full of cheering fans more inspiring than games away from their own turf? After all, some professional athletes are paid millions of dollars to employ their skills. Perhaps it is the adrenalin rush that comes from the cheerleaders or fans, or perhaps it is as simple as knowing that they are not alone; others care about what they are doing too. Whatever the reason, you can intuitively understand that having others at your side helps.

If you find others diminish your efforts, then you dismiss their attitude and carry on. After all, at the end of the day it is **you** who must decide if it is helpful, harmful, or a misguided effort. I, for one, firmly believe that most forms of self-exploration embellish our humanity and result in us being even better than before.

Let us see the world more clearly, as Copernicus did, let us see our world as astutely as Einstein did, and let us understand ourselves as bravely as Freud did.

2
EMOTION REGULATION

Emotions, feelings, and affect are synonymous. Everyone has emotions. Sometimes they are helpful and sometimes they are hurtful. The academic study of emotions is an attempt to find out why this is so, and how to identify what factors are important in changing emotions when we should or want to, and how to embellish the ones that serve us well. Mesquita et. al,. (2014) writes "Having an emotion means to take a stance, to have a particular relationship with the world (Soloman, 2004), and to have a specific intention to act (Frijda, 1986)." Gross (2014) defines emotion regulation as "shaping which emotions one has, when one has them, and how one experiences or expresses these emotions." He further states that emotions "direct attention to key features of the environment, optimize key sensory intake, tune decision making, ready behavioral responses, facilitate social interaction, and enhance episodic memory." The academic study of emotion regulation has been going on for 35 years (Zimmerman & Thompson, 2014). Scholars have learned a great deal over the last 35 years about the topic, and it is relevant to review some of their ideas and findings, because, as Gross—a leader in the field—says "we are both governed by—and governors of—our emotions."

Table 1 shows some of the critical functions of emotions and emotion regulation.

Table 1	
• emotional learning	• balance priorities
• shapes what we expect	• improves decision making
• helps bonding in relationships	• assists in forming our beliefs
• helps us develop goals	• assists in defining what situations we place ourselves in
• defines how we value situations	
• how to modify our situations	• frequently informs us how to react
• shapes anticipations of the future	• gets our attention
	• helps us make choices
• creates behavioral scripts we follow	• can soothe or irritate
	• directs our attention
• creates self-evaluations	• buffer distress and stress

It can be seen that Emotion Regulation has a lot to offer. We will examine many of the functions of Emotion Regulation below, using both the terms scholars use and the more vernacular.

Attention

You have all been told, perhaps many times, "pay attention," as if attention is a unitary concept when in fact the role of attention is multifaceted. First, if someone claps their hands in a crowded room you would guess they want your attention. But really what occurs first is an orienting reflex, "What is that about?" That is different than concentrated attention. What if in your history your father always clapped his hands (to get your attention) prior to giving you a spanking? When you are in the crowded room and someone claps their hands you might be likely to experience fearful anticipation, not attention. Environments themselves can be designed to focus your attention (such as in a classroom or concert hall where all the chairs are faced in one direction, toward the teacher or orchestra). But even here the classroom may not be effective in directing your attention (if you are more socially motivated rather than academically motivated, the desks and chairs are opportunities for you to whisper to your classmate, pass silly notes, or *get* attention from other than the teacher).

Sustained attention requires many elements, as Johnstone and Walter (2014) point out: "...detecting and appraising situations and contexts that call for certain emotional responses (e.g., threat detection, relevance detection, recognition of socially rewarding stimuli, evaluation of possible outcomes and their probabilities..." can all influence your emotion regulation strategies as well as "paying attention."

Conscious awareness of what you are attending to and why is thus a critical element of emotion regulation. There can be sustained attention (as in mindfulness or meditation), fleeting attention (as when you are flipping the channels on your TV to get to the station you really want to watch), obsessive attention (as when most major networks showed the 9/11 attack on the twin towers), ruminative attention (as when the boyfriend checks his phone every two minutes to see if his proposed new girlfriend will text him back), and lack of attention (as when you left your cheese sandwich on the grill burning and decide to take a short walk on a nice day). Emotional vulnerability has been attributed, in part, to biased attentional selectivity (MacLeod & Grafton, 2014), or in other words paying attention to the wrong things. Attention deployment is thus a critical element of emotion regulation (Gross, 2014).

Rumination (thinking about the same thing over and over,

but not having a strategy or purpose to your attention) has been shown to potentially have very negative outcomes (Sheppes, 2014). Rumination may be viewed as deploying your attention in circles, purposelessly. Sounds bad, and it is. But most of us will admit there have been many times we engage in rumination. We do it sometimes because the stakes are high (will a loved one live through an accident or illness), and sometimes the importance is low (did I remember to turn off the TV before I left the house). If rumination serves few useful functions, why do we do it? Perhaps because attention and valuation are so intertwined.

Takeaway: Having some control over your attention, noticing it, is important. You increase your emotional vulnerability, distress, by paying too little attention or too much attention, or attending to the wrong things.

Valuation

Valuation refers to how important you find something. As such it is an assessment, sometimes conscious and sometimes without awareness (LeDoux, 2000). Researchers call it valence, the "goodness or badness, desirability or undesirability, pleasure or pain" (Jones, Kirkland, & Cunningham, 2014). But valence (Russell, 2003) is not just about a judgment or thought, it is also about how you feel (Västfjäl et. al, 2016) about that judgment. We constantly evaluate the value of any event, situation, or process. Based upon these thoughts, we have feelings. All kinds of things determine how we value things: immediacy (are you in immediate danger or likely to get immediate reward), proximity (will Johnny, who is two years old, get in to a good college is far away; did I get my keys before I locked the door is something that may need attending to soon), identity (how closely the event accords with how you see yourself), relevance (is this going to happen to you, or to someone else?), and social comparison (the keep up with the Jones' phenomenon as well as family and cultural expectations).

How you valuate also involves how much weight you assign to it. Dropping a pen as you get out of the car has much less significance to you than if you accidentally run over your neighbor's dog.

Some scholars refer to hedonic influences (e.g., Mauss & Tamir, 2014) in valuation as opposed to eudaimonic (e.g., Ryan & Deci, 2001). The hedonic approach basically describes Freud's pleasure principle (we seek pleasure and avoid pain). The eudaimonic approach refers to pursuit of happiness and meaning, rather than simply pursuing pleasure (Huta, 2016).

Takeaway: Look to your values and your feelings.

Risk Assessments, Attributions and Misattributions

Attributions are related to but distinct from valuations. While a valuation is how important we see an event or process, an attribution is what we think about the event or process. Further, it is a mental representation. You may misattribute foul intents for my purpose in writing this workbook. This makes you feel annoyed. If someone then insists you read and work the book or they will leave the relationship with you, you may see the entire situation as a threat (your risk assessment).

Researchers like to divide emotions into two large groups: integral affect and incidental affect (Västfjäl et. al, 2016). Integral affect (also called endogenous emotions) helps us to evaluate good from bad (Kahneman et al., 1997) and are based on an identifiable situation or event, while incidental affect (also called exogenous emotions) is when you form your feelings based on moods or irrelevant information. Misattribution (ascribing a characteristic or quality that is not there) most frequently comes from incidental affect.

Attributions are exceptionally important to goal-directed behavior: the ability to skillfully strategize, human relationships, the adhesiveness of our cultures, and our ability to prolong happiness and truncate anguish. This is so due to the fact that an attribution (the qualities we ascribe to something) will predict our appraisal of threat, our approach or avoidance to a situation, and our estimations about success (self-esteem and perseverance).

Most people know about the "fight or flight" response. In order to engage the process we have to detect a threat (real or imagined). Threat detection, or risk assessments, can be automatic (controlled by lower brain areas without conscious awareness) or thoughtful (controlled by higher brain areas with awareness). That is one of the reasons why attribution theory and research is so important. Just think of some potential unwanted consequences of misattribution:

- you flee from potentially rewarding relationships
- you do not go to college because you think you are not smart enough
- you are in college but don't study for a test because you think you are smart
- you quit your job (that you like) because you dislike your new supervisor
- you tell your new supervisor how much you dislike them and get fired
- you binge watch TV because at least you can feel safe
- you fail to leave the house for days because you are in a bad mood

- you play video games on your phone for hours rather than talking to friends
- you fail to make friends because you think you are unlikable
- you spend money at the store you don't have, hoping it will make you happy
- you spend all weekend returning clothes "because they just don't fit"

The ability to appropriately focus your attention, to recognize your values and feelings, to acknowledge attributions and misattributions—and to shift from one strategy to different one when a previous one failed to accomplish your goal all depend on how skillfully you use all of the above processes. This is emotion regulation.

Takeaway: Don't form judgments without all the information about both the situation and your values.

Two Ways of Feeling: Bottom-Up and Top-Down

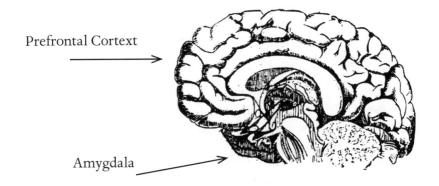

Prefrontal Cortext

Amygdala

Figure 3 Two Ways of Feeling

The brain above shows two ways of feeling: top-down (going from the prefrontal cortex down to the amygdala) and bottom-up (going from the amygdala up to the prefrontal cortex). Each produces a different experience. The prefrontal cortex area of the brain houses what are called "executive functions" (thinking, planning, and executing action). Interestingly, the prefrontal cortex is believed to be one of the last areas of the brain to historically develop, and then it is one of the last area of the brain to fully mature. The amygdala is the "emotion brain." Here we have a feeling sensation without any thought. Examples include the startle response, fear, rage, and sometimes anger (bottom-up). To complicate things you can think of a time when within a split second of having a startle response you recognized there were no reasons to be startled and settled down. Within that split second your prefrontal lobe had time to process or think through the experience. Or a time when you had plenty of time to think about all the reasons you were angry (top-down). These two areas do work collaboratively, but offer many complications to human life as well.

As Johnstone and Walter (2014) point out, there are very few neural pathways from the limbic system (that includes the amygdala) to the prefrontal cortex. Since there are less "highways" from the emotion centers and the thinking centers of the brain, that means that with very strong feelings the highways get jammed and "movement" can take some time. We recover from trauma slowly, requiring soothing and safety-seeking behaviors. The amygdala also seems to have "memory" of its own, apart from the conscious thoughts from the prefrontal cortex. Very strong emotions, especially those we do not fully understand, can linger and cause enduring unhappiness. But there is hope, as there are many good therapists and books based upon experimental research and we clinicians know offer successful resolution.

This brief explanation of the brain is a glittering oversimplification. In fact there are a plethora of brain areas involved in the emotions

(Ocher & Gross, 2014; Johnstone & Walter, 2014). While we know much more today than when I went to graduate school 40 years ago, we continue to learn more about brain functioning every day.

We know we want to down-regulate negative emotions (where the literature demonstrates higher activity in the prefrontal cortex and lower in the amygdala (Proudfit et al., 2014)) and up-regulate positive emotions (to feel good and not feel bad).

The fact that we have a complicated emotional network system is not a bad thing. As philosophers centuries ago remarked, combining reason and emotion is a lifelong task. And life would be pretty dull without emotions; we would be computer robots and not fully human.

Takeaway: Feelings are complicated. Try to think and feel.

Emotions and Physical Health

The relationship between repetitive or long-term feelings and physical health problems has been long known (Walker, Sharpe & Wessley, 2006). And we know from medical cost offset data that every dollar spent on mental health results in reduction in medical costs (Anderson & Estee, 2002). Why? Many emotional problems, especially if chronic, cause a corresponding increase in medical care utilization. People get physically sick due to their emotions.

This research area (health and emotions) is broad, extensive, scary, and offers insight in to why it is important to regulate our emotions. For example, an inability to discuss angry feelings predicts heart disease (Hanes, Feinleb & Kannel, 1980). Another study showed a 20% to 60% less probability of developing heart disease with the ability to regulate emotions (Kubzansky et al., 2011). Other health problems such as infectious disease and the common cold (Cohen, Tyrrell, & Smith, 1993), declines in lung function (Kubzansky et al., 2006) diabetes (Mezuk, Eaton, Albrecht, & Golden, 2008), arthritis (Karakus & Patton, 2011), and cancer (Kroenke et al., 2006) have been reported.

This section relies heavily on one excellent review (DeSterno, Gross, and Kubzansky, 2013).

Takeaway: Protect your physical health by regulating your emotions.

Fortunately, there are many strategies and techniques (such as reappraisal, attention training, shifting strategies between short-term and long-term goals, increasing positive emotions, decreasing negative emotions, value enhancement, contextual recognition, relationship enhancement, balancing strategies, and others) that all are covered in this workbook. All of the strategies, when used together, are designed to decrease your distress and increase your happiness.

MINDFULNESS

Why a chapter on mindfulness in a workbook on how to deal with decreasing unwanted emotions, and increasing desired ones? The ability to bring to bear mindfulness to your environment, body, feelings, and relationships is critical.

Our 'training,' so to speak, begins in utero. The unborn child hears the voices and sounds even before birth. The mother affectionately rubs her belly, and all the family surround her with "oohs" and "awes." The unborn baby is welcomed in the world. When the baby is born it already knows mama's voice. It distantly knows daddy's voice too. These sounds, especially the welcomed ones, overshadow the trauma of being thrust out of the womb to the world. Then the miracle of life continues, after the screams and crying comes the comfort, and the bind between child and mother (Bowlby, 1969) begins.

So what has this have to do with mindfulness? *Senses* begin before birth. And they are powerful. Let's get simple. Senses are part of feelings. And feelings are real, even if they cannot yet be described.

DEFINITION OF MINDFULNESS

Mindfulness is sensing, observing, in this moment, without analysis. That in and of itself is difficult (see below). Mindfulness is the opposite of mindlessness. With mindlessness you complete a task to get the task done. With mindfulness you attempt to experience (use your senses consciously and with focus) whenever you are doing something. Mindfulness is not a task, it is a process. The process of observing you're doing, the interaction of your doing with the object, and observing which of the five senses you use in the observing. It is watchful. It is the opposite of distraction (Kabat-Zinn, 1982). You watch what you see, hear, taste, touch, and smell. You attempt to experience it rather than think about it.

Differences Between Mindfulness and Just Paying Attention

Two major differences between paying attention and mindful meditation are that you are attending to a broader array of perceptions (external, internal, and the interaction of the two) resulting in reperceiving the world (Farb et al., 2014). Second, you are able to separate yourself as observer and that which is observed. In semantics this difference is noted by the phrase "the map is not the territory" (Hayakawa & Hayakawa, 1991) which means that both our perceptions and the words we use to describe an event or experience are not the same as the experience or event itself. While this may seem like splitting hairs, it is not.

Many of our attentional difficulties, misperceptions, and goal-oriented problem solving tasks can be off base precisely because we do not differentiate our perception from the object perceived. Because I think you are a louse does not make you a louse. Because I feel worthless does not make me worthless. Because I see doom and gloom does not mean doom and gloom exist.

Under high emotionality, your thinking can follow your feelings.

Or the reverse, your feeling can influence your thinking. This knowledge, if applied, can make tremendous difference in your life, as the following Figure shows:

	Situation	Attention	Appraisal	Response
Conventional Stress Response	Solve Problematic Emotion ⇨	External/ Historical Stressor ⇨	Reduced Quality of Life ⇨	Sadness Anger & Frustration
Mindful Stress Response	Explore Nature of Emotion ⇨	External/ Historical Stressor Momentary Sensation ⇨	Transitory Challenge Opportunity for Insight ⇨	Curiosity & Acceptance
	...Intention...	...Attention...	...Attitude...	...Attitude...

Figure 4: Differences Between Conventional and Mindful Stress Responses
Permission granted by Farb (Farb, Anderson, Irving, and Segal, 2014)

Figure 4 shows that in the situation you are stressed. Without using mindfulness you try to solve the problem, and your attention is focused on the problem, resulting in your appraisal that you are unhappy because you have a problem to solve (perhaps sadness, anger or frustration). In the same situation using mindfulness you see a situation (a stressor) and explore your emotions associated with the situation, your attention is focused on the stressor as a momentary sensation, which leads to an attitude that this is a transitory situation resulting in curiosity. So the difference with mindful coping with emotions is that it is characterized by exploration, curiosity, feelings are accurately defined as momentary and fleeting.

Feelings change, naturally. When they don't it is due to one of two reasons: it is biologically based (as in schizophrenias, bipolar disorder, or autism spectrum disorders) or there are maintaining factors in your environment that prompt, regenerate, and sustain your feelings. The latter we will deal with later in this workbook.

WHY IS MINDFULNESS SO DIFFICULT?

If mindfulness is nothing more than coming back to your senses, then why do so many of us have difficulty sustaining it, for even brief moments? Let's go back to infancy. We begin with sounds. Our vision in the beginning is blurry. We begin with pronouns: "Mama." (If you are lucky, a healthy dose of comfort is provided.) We graduate to vocabulary. This is your mouth, this is your finger, this is your leg, and so on. A baby has an incredible ability to quickly learn to capture and store in memory a tremendous vocabulary. Then comes yet another graduation, beyond caregiver and self. We begin to see a world beyond self and caregiver. We learn colors, we name them. Trees, we name them. Grass, we name it. And very special, water, we bathe in it.

Watching a baby in bathwater is a learning moment in mindfulness for the infant (and for us adults): It is there, I can touch it, but it is fluid, I can't grasp it. The baby is awe struck. It is there. I can see it. I can touch it. I can't grasp it. But wait, I can slash it! And the baby smiles and laughs as they splash the water. And splash and splash. Glee, pure excitement, joy, wonder, amazement. This is mindfully being with water.

Over time we squash this mindful glee. The adult might say, "Okay Julie, bath time is almost over. Wipe yourself off. We do not have all day." Bath time is no longer an exploratory experience; it becomes a task. The purpose of a bath is to get clean, not to play, not to experience the world.

Or the baby in his car seat points through the window and says gleefully "tree." Dad is exuberant, "Yes, Adam that is a tree!" Later it becomes, "Adam, do you have your seatbelt on? Can you stop making mouth noises? Daddy is trying to drive." Ever so quickly the child is told that the task is what is important, and they are subtly told that play is disapproved of, and they are not being "good" when they continue to desire to explore the world with awe and curiosity.

Just one step further. The child goes to school, and the elementals of the scientific approach are taught. First, like in infancy, we name. But we have a fancier name for it, we call it nomenclature. Then, we categorize. Grass, trees, plants, and shrubs are all botanicals. Flies, mosquitos, ticks, and spiders are all insects. Cows, sheep, horses, and pigs are all animals. We no longer have to pay much attention to the individual thing (the idiographic), we can now conveniently use the category (the nomothetic).

That is a great thing for science. But what is lost when a child is no longer rewarded for noticing how tall the tree is, how green the leaves are, how dark the bark is, and (with imagination) how deeply the roots of tree grow in the earth to draw both moisture and nutrients (bringing a face blush to D. H. Lawrence who so wonderfully describes the same experience in his literature)? What is lost is experience. We think about things and don't observe them with the same focus, the same intensity, the same full-of-care delight and contentment we use to have. That is a great loss.

So mindfulness, which comes naturally as sensual beings, is trained out of us. By everybody. Just another unforeseen consequence of progress, or our obsessions with task completion. The benefits are many (socially, sociologically, economically, and politically). And the costs are dramatic as well (we stop feeling and spend too much time in our head) as we diminish a very important aspect of what it means to be human.

BENEFITS OF MINDFULNESS

Look at what the scholars have to say. In Table 2 I've compiled a list of benefits that Davis and Hayes (2011) reviewed. Both researchers and practitioners have reported other and overlapping benefits, including increased access to senses, decreased rumination, and increased attentional stability (Farb et al., 2014). Who doesn't want better self-control, to be more objective about life, to tolerate the good and the bad better, to be more flexible in our thinking, to concentrate better, or to feel less anxiety? We all want those things! And with the increasing body of literature on the health benefits of mindfulness (like increased immune functioning, reduced medical symptoms, decreased experienced pain) we should be salivating like Pavlov's dogs to get it now.

Yet, there are costs. The cost is not in a pill or a doctor visit. It is time and effort. Because mindfulness is free, it is in the public domain, it is available to you right now. Pay the price of your time and effort.

Table1: Benefits of Mindfulness	
Benefit	**Scholarly Research To Support It**
Self-Control	Bishop et al., 2004; Masicampo & Baumeister, 2007
Objectivity	Adele & Feldman, 2004; Brown & Croswell, 2007; Leary & Tate, 2007; Shapiro et al., 2006
Affect Tolerance	Fulton, 2005
Enhanced Flexibility	Adele & Feldman, 2004

Equanimity	Morgan & Morgan, 2005
Improved Concentration and Mental Clarity	Young, 1997
Emotional Intelligence	Walsh & Shapiro, 2006
Relate to Self With Kindness, Acceptance, and Compassion	Fulton, 2005; Wallace, 2001
State of Awareness	Siegel, 2007
Better Focus of Attention	Cahn & Polich, 2009
Affect Regulation Cognitive Flexibility	Wallin, 2007; Moore & Malinowski, 2009
Emotion Regulation	Cocoran et al., 2010; Farb et al., 2010; Siegel, 2007
Reduced Anxiety Reduced Rumination Reduced Medical Symptoms	Chambers et al, 2008
Reduced Emotional Reactivity	Farb et al., 2010
Actual Brain Changes As A Result of Mindfulness	Williams, 2010
Increased Immune Functioning	Davidson et al., 2003

MINDFULNESS EXERCISES

Since mindfulness is a process and not an outcome, we have to start at the beginning. Even if you have done this before, please follow these instructions. It is always best to start at the beginning and then progress.

Sustaining Attention To The Environment

What To Do: Pick a Handy Object
Spend 3 minutes describing the object with your senses.

Why To Do It: It will remind you how
we get lost in our own words.
It will demonstrate how difficult focused attention is.

How To Do It: If you can't find something
handy, pick from the following list.

Potential objects:

- Pencil
- Business Card
- Safety Pen
- Paper Clip
- Rubber Band
- Cell phone, turned off
- Checkbook
- Eyeglass cleaners
- Prescription bottle
- Cough drop

- Credit card
- Ruler
- Water bottle

Remember Your Senses:

- Vision (Sight)
- Hearing (Auditory)
- Touch (Tactile)
- Smell (Olfactory)
- Taste (Gustatory)

After choosing your object, devote at least three minutes to describing it using your senses.

Not: "It is a 24 pound single piece of copy paper made by Swenton Avenue Trading, Inc., in Baton Raton FL and 99.99% jam free." That would be naming, not describing from experience.

Example

If you really do this exercise, most find a loss of words. "It is just a simple piece of paper!" There is a compulsion to naming and dismissing. To move on. To not experience. Give that piece of paper to *my* dog, who does not have expectations or preconceived beliefs, and he will react differently: His behavior will be as if to say, "Wow, what is this? Let me taste it. Let me claw it to pieces. Let me shuffle it all over the room. Let me play with it. Let me have some fun with it." The dog will experience it, not analyze it or think and ponder about it. If even for a short time, he will "become one with the paper."

So what? Well, if at the end of the day you say to yourself "I made 18 sales today." Or "I changed the baby's diaper 9 times today." Or worse, "Gosh, what did I really accomplish today?" You have missed experience. I garden not just because I enjoy beautiful flowers, but because I enjoy the experience of dirt on my hands, the care for the seeds I plant, the anticipation of after I water what will eventually happen. Yes, the product is a flower, which I very much enjoy, but I enjoy the communal experience of the earth, the seed or bulb, the water, the sun and warmth, the growing process itself. That, in my mind, is even as beautiful as the flower itself. Hopefully you feel the same way about your marriage, your children, your business, your coworkers, your neighbors, your political endeavors, your trip planning…and your own life.

MINDFULNESS TO BODY

It is hard enough to focus on the environment without dismissing it by simply naming it. There are many other dimensions to mindfulness. In physics it is called "the observation effect" (Weizmann, 1998). Grandma probably put it more simply. "A watched kettle does not boil." What do these things mean? You can't separate the observed from the observer. Sometimes a book title says it all. You don't necessarily have to read the entire book to get the point. Kabat-Zinn wrote (2005) "Where Ever You Go There You Are." In order to fully understand what is outside of us, we must explore what is inside of us. The simplest way is to start with our own body.

If we wish to fully come back to our senses, we need to feel the sensor itself. We know the five senses. We try to more fully use them. We start our exploration with just a few of them.

Mindfulness to Breath

We breathe. We always do, or we die. The breath is a monumental tool so frequently ignored. Since it is automatic we don't think of it. If we have a panic attack, begin to hyperventilate, the natural course of our biology is to "reset" the system. We pass out. Then we go back to auto pilot and survive. We breathe normally again.

Let's go to a less extreme example. You are so focused on your task that frustration and irritability increases. Your breathing becomes short and shallow. You are stressed. Some of us will, as a result, *increase* our attention to the task, to jam a result (an outcome) from the environment.

A different approach would be self-awareness. Watching our breath as a measure of our stress, and adjusting accordingly. "I'm frustrated. I can feel it in my breathing."

Try this exercise when you are feeling okay. Try it again when you are not feeling okay.

What to Do: Follow your breath

Why To Do It: It can bring calm
It focuses your attention on self
It can interrupt constant internal chatter
(your never-ending thoughts)

How To Do It: Follow the rhythm of your breath
Notice your chest (lungs inflate and deflate)
Feel the air coming in and out of your nose
Notice temperature, notice as much as you can

Example: I feel my breath coming in through my nose, I feel a brief pause, I feel my exhale leaving my body, I feel a brief pause. My chest and stomach move slightly during each breath. I'm aware that my breath strokes feel longer and deeper, as I feel the air entering, then a pause, and leaving. The air in my nostrils feels cooler than the air as it exits. I feel the in, and out. The chest rising and falling, subtly. In and out, I feel relaxed. In and out.

Try to do this for three minutes before you stop. And notice when you practice mindful breathing when you are relaxed, and how it is different when you become stressed. Notice the differences. Notice when extraneous thoughts (thoughts about the past, the future, or other thoughts not having to do with your breathing). Bring your attention back to your breathing.

Other Kinds of Mindfulness

For the same reasons, try some of the following strategies. Notice that you can do many of these things every day. The effort is to be mindful, and the object of your mindfulness is less important.

Table 3
Other Forms of Mindfulness

	What To Pay Attention To
Mindful Walking	Your gait, weight, balance, body movements, stride
Mindful of the Sun and Wind	Close your eyes on a sunny day and look upwards Feel the temperature, light through your eyelids Feel the wind, and how it changes the temperature
Mindfulness of Music	Pick an instrumental piece, close your eyes and try to identify each instrument as it plays, how the

	instruments complement each other, and the rhythm of the sounds (soft, loud, sweet, disharmonious or harmonious)
Mindfulness With Aromas	Go to a cosmetic counter and smell each bottle of cologne or perfume; many health food stores have aromatherapy shelves (try cinnamon, eucalyptus, lemon, vanilla, or your favorite one)
Tactile Focus	Pay attention when you bathe or shower Use an invigorating body shampoo Try different hair shampoo scents, and notice any difference
Visual Sensations	Stair at a photograph (National Geographic is a good choice), notice the background and the foreground, the colors and the textures, or look out your favorite window and notice both what moves and that which does not

These techniques of mindfulness are more fully explored elsewhere (Marra, 2004). Once you feel confidence that you can stick with your observations (sustain your attention), when your observations are about the moment and what you sense (not what you think), then begin to shift your attention back and forth between the object observed, and your body reactions to that observation.

You Are Not Done

Mindfulness needs to become a way of life rather than an activity from which you "graduate." If you are a religious person, you would not tell your Reverend (Priest, Rabi, Deacon, Alim, Grand Mufi, etc) "No problem, I've got myself covered. I pray here with you almost every time." Like prayer, you have to practice mindfulness. You are never done with it.

KEEP A JOURNAL

There are many reasons to keep a journal, to actually write things down. It prompts you to do it. If you look at your journal and there are no entries for a week, you know you are slipping back to your old ways of being in the world. You can look back at your entries and notice those things you did that brought satisfaction, internal quiet and peace, those that were vivid and successful for you, and thus things that you want to repeat. Finally, it is part of *reflection*: taking stock of your experiences. Writing takes time, and slowing down this experience in our task-oriented lifestyles can be helpful.

**What to Do: Keep a Journal, Complete
the form at least once a day**

**Why To Do It: Establishes routine or habit of mindful living
Causes you to reflect on your experiences**

**How To Do It: Write the date in the top box
Find the sense that matched your practice and write in that box**

Example: Date – **Wednesday**   **Thursday**

Sound—Opened window and listened to the birds chirp for 5 min.

Tactile—Mindfully pet my dog 5 min.

Taste-- Mindfully ate my fish and spinach ate slowly, tasted each bite, paused between each forkful

Visual – Looked at flowers mindfully

Date		
Smell		
Tactile		
Visual		
Sound		

Taste		

You will find clean worksheets at the end of the book; photocopy them and use them frequently.

4
FEELINGS

Feelings may be fluid experiences, changing from moment to moment. Most would agree that, along with thoughts and visceral (body) experience, they all comprise the building blocks of what we call our humanity. They have made sci-fi movies about societies that prohibit the populace from feeling (through drugs), from discussing them (through brainwashing), and from using them in daily life (through social control). While it makes for a good movie, it would be a world devoid of the vividness and inspiration we now take for granted. What are feelings or emotions?

While it is easy to say emotions are simple, "I feel happy," feelings are related to but more than senses. Given a normal birth, we sense very early in life. The infant does not yet know the word 'hungry' but will take the breast or bottle to feed. But she can't say 'sad' or 'hurt' or 'angry' until much later. It is the interplay, interaction, and summation of the following elements that bring what we come to know as a feeling:

- visceral (body): tight or relaxed muscles, fast or slow breathing, senses "fight, flight, or delight"
- cognitive (brain): your thoughts about what you experience, as well as the important roles of attributions, anticipation and beliefs
- genetic makeup (provides a set point or baseline for arousal)
- social (how we are trained to respond to threat, meaning, and survival)

THE BIOPSYCHOSOCIAL MODEL OF EMOTIONS

Although feelings are given great weight in society (after all, they are the basis of bonding, our communal behaviors, and our willingness (or not) to comply with societal expectations), most of us don't stop to tease apart what prompts or creates them. That kind of information is critical to regulating them (make the good ones stay, and the bad ones go away).

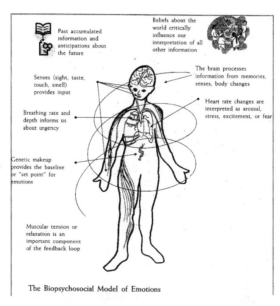

Figure 5: The Biopsychosocial Model of Emotions

THE BIOPSYCHOSOCIAL MODEL OF EMOTIONS

As Figure 5 above demonstrates, the biopsychosocial model of emotions assumes that each element (biology, psychology, and environment) reciprocally influence each other in establishing our total experience of the world. For example, when our heart rate increases the body can interpret this as a sign of danger, and as a result the body tightens muscles in preparation for fight or flight. We will be more likely to interpret sensory input (sight, sound, touch, and taste) as signals of such danger. We begin to breathe rapidly and shallowly. We remember similar threats experienced in the past, and connect with assumptions about the world (do we see it as a supportive or threatening place?) The swirl indicates that each component influences each of the others. If we wish to reduce crisis and tension, we can increase body relaxation, shift our input from the environment to those that are supportive, and reinterpret our assumptions and thoughts. The model predicts great hope that we can influence our emotions since there are so many levels we can begin to change.

NAMING FEELINGS

Let's start with a short list of feelings:

Anger
Anxiety
Futility
Joy
Happiness
Satisfaction
Exhilaration

How are anger and joy alike, and how are they different? With anger your muscles can be tense (as in ready to punch someone), but also with joy (as in jumping for joy). With both there is arousal (ready to attack or to embrace). With both your breathing can change, your experience is heightened, but in one case it feels bad and in the other it feels good.

We know the prompting event makes all the difference. If you (the environment) criticize me (self) again, I feel angry. If you (environment) tell me (self) you are marrying the love of your life, I feel joy.

So you know all this already. Then why can't you make good feelings linger and bad feelings go away? If you know your husband Joe is the cause (the prompting events) of most of your anger, then why don't you change it? Maybe you could write page after page of all the things Joe does that infuriates you. But you don't change it (remove yourself from the situation, with great clarity inform him how he repeatedly upsets you, or get a different Joe in your life?). Because you love him. He makes you feel ill but you love him. And what about Joe? Unless you are an unassertive doormat you probably have told him multiple times, for years, why he makes you angry. Why doesn't Joe take the initiative and leave you? Probably for the same reason; he loves you.

VALUES

I love my husband more than I hate him. I love my wife more than I hate her. I love my parents, but they are hard on me. My neighbor is a pain, but I've known him for ten years. My professor is stingy with compliments, but I learn from her. That baby is driving me nuts, but boy do I love him and he is so cute. My boyfriend is selfish and self-centered, but he listens to me. My pastor is erratic and demanding, but I love his sermons. My sister is stupid, but she is the only sister I have. This house is old and in need of constant repairs, but I can't even imagine living anywhere else.

FEELING WORDS

First we start with feeling names, and determine their frequency, intensity, and personal value. This is not simple self-exploration, for later we will use this same information in order to increase positive emotions, and decrease emotions you don't like.

What To Do: Read the list of feelings and complete the chart

**Why To Do It: Assess your everyday
experience more closely than normally
Give thought to your values (Is this good, or bad, for me?;
Is this harmful or helpful to me?)**

**How To Do It: Study the ranking schemes below.
Read the feeling word. Ask yourself how
frequently you feel that emotion.
How intense is that emotion? It if you feel
bothered daily, but it is not a hassle for you at all,
then probably it not need be attended to.**

Frequency	Intensity
1--I hardly ever feel it.	1 – It is miniscule, hardly notice it.
2—I feel it daily.	2—I notice it, but it does not interfere.
3—I feel it more than once a day.	3 – It is bothersome.
4- I feel it innumerable times per day.	4—I'm really worried about it. It interferences with what I'm doing.

5—I feel it constantly, overwhelmingly.

5—It is so intense I find it difficult to function.

Value:
Do you want this
in your life?

Even feelings that most think of as positive, like love, can have an intensity of 5

Yes

_____

_____

_____

No

_____

_____

_____

What To Do: Identify your most frequent
and intense undesired emotions.

Why To Do It: You will be better prepared to analyze
prompting events for unwanted emotions.

How To Do It: Place a check mark next to
the feelings with a Frequency of 4 or 5 _and_ an
Intensity of 4 or 5 _and_ are Valued as No.

Example:

Feeling	Intensity	Frequency	Valued
Angry	4	5	No
Annoyed	4	2	No

Resentful	2	3	No
Remorseful	2	2	Yes
Restless	1	1	No
Sad	5	3	No
Scared	5	4	No
Serious	5	5	Yes
Shy	1	1	No
Sarcastic	1	1	No
Thankful	3	4	Yes
Tired	3	4	No
Tranquil	1	1	Yea
Worried	5	5	No
Hatred	1	1	No
Lonely	4	5	No
Desperate	2	4	No
Confused	1	1	No
Numb	1	1	No
Panic	3	1	No
Fearful	4	5	No
Anguish	3	3	No
Anxiety	4	3	No
Rage	1	2	No
Empty/Wanting	3	3	No
Disgusted	1	3	No
Cheerful	1	1	Yes
Loved	3	4	Yes
Enthusiastic	1	1	Yes
Joy	1	1	Yes
Mirth	1	1	Yes
Amused	2	3	Yes
Delighted	3	2	Yes

Giddy	1	1	No
Laughter	2	3	Yes
Romantic	3	3	Yes
Serenity	1	1	Yes
Gratitude	1	1	No
Euphoria	1	1	No
Pride	2	2	No
Awe	3	3	Yes
Resentful	3	3	No
Remorseful	3	3	No
Restless	2	3	No
Sad	3	2	No
Scared	4	4	No
Serious	4	3	Yes
Shy	1	1	No
Sarcastic	2	2	No
Thankful	3	3	Yes
Tired	3	3	No
Tranquil	1	1	Yes
Worried	4	3	No
Hatred	1	3	No
Lonely	2	3	No
Desperate	1	1	No
Confused	1	1	No
Numb	1	1	No
Panic	1	1	No
Fearful	3	3	No
Anguish	2	3	No
Anxiety	2	3	No
Rage	2	4	No
Empty/Wanting	3	4	No

Disgusted	1	3	No
Other Frequent:			

We can see from the above example that the most frequent desired emotion (those rated with a frequency of 4 or 5, and an intensity of 4 or 5) is desired. Similarly, for the undesired emotions (those not valued) the feelings are angry, worried, scared, lonely, and fearful. Now you rate your own feelings:

FEELING	INTENSITY	FREQUENCY	VALUE
Resentful			
Remorseful			
Restless			
Sad			
Scared			
Serious			
Shy			
Sarcastic			
Thankful			
Tired			
Tranquil			
Worried			
Hatred			
Lonely			
Desperate			
Confused			
Numb			
Panic			
Fearful			
Anguish			
Anxiety			
Rage			

Empty/Wanting _____ _____ _____

Disgusted _____ _____ _____

Serenity _____ _____ _____

Gratitude _____ _____ _____

Euphoria _____ _____ _____

Pride _____ _____ _____

Awe _____ _____ _____

Cheerful _____ _____ _____

Loved _____ _____ _____

Enthusiastic _____ _____ _____

Joy _____ _____ _____

Mirth _____ _____ _____

Amused _____ _____ _____

Delighted _____ _____ _____

Giddy _____ _____ _____

Laughter _____ _____ _____

Romantic _____ _____ _____

Serenity _____ _____ _____

Gratitude _____ _____ _____

Euphoria _____ _____ _____

Pride _____ _____ _____

Awe _____ _____ _____

Cheerful _____ _____ _____

Loved _____ _____ _____

Enthusiastic _____ _____ _____

Joy _____ _____ _____

Mirth _____ _____ _____

Amused _____ _____ _____

Delighted _____ _____ _____

Giddy _____ _____ _____

Laughter _____ _____ _____

Romantic _____ _____ _____

Serenity			
Gratitude			
Euphoria			
Restless			
Sad			
Scared			
Serious			
Shy			
Sarcastic			
Thankful			
Tired			
Tranquil			
Worried			
Hatred			
Lonely			
Desperate			
Confused			
Numb			
Panic			
Fearful			
Anguish			
Anxiety			
Rage			
Empty/Wanting			
Disgusted			
Restless			
Sad			
Scared			

After you have completed your ratings, place a check mark next to the feelings with a Frequency of 4 or 5 *and* an Intensity of 4 or 5 *and* are Valued as No. Make sure each of the three conditions are met for your check mark. Write those feelings down in the following chart in the first row of each column. Now think of the situations (what is going on at the time) that create those feelings.

Examples:

Feelings	Situations That Make Me Feel That Way
Angry	- When my son disobeys my directions
	- When my spouse forgets to go to the store and we just talked about it before I came home
	- When I'm the only one who cleans up after the dog
Fearful	- When I hear news reports about drug use at schools, and I worry my son will join in with the crowd
	- When I'm watching the news and there is a big traffic jam and my spouse is late coming home
	- When the TV does not work and I miss the news
	- When my son tells me he hates my guts and he wants a different parent
Lonely	- When my kids at school, spouse at work, and everyone I try to telephone it just goes in to their voicemail
Scared	- When I'm alone in the dark
	- When I hear noises in the back yard
	- When the telephone rings and I'm not expecting a call
	- When my heart starts racing and I'm afraid I'll have a heart attack

I understand this task is difficult, and you may have to ponder the many circumstances you are in that prompts your feelings. It may take more than one or two sittings to complete this. An additional blank form is provided in the back of the book. Work just this part of the exercise as many times as necessary.

What To Do: Identify your most frequent and less intense undesired emotions.

Why To Do It: You will be better prepared to analyze prompting events for unwanted emotions.

How To Do It: Place a check mark next to the feelings with a Frequency of 4 or 5 _and_ an Intensity of 4 or 5 _and_ are Valued as No.

We will return to your work in the assignment above in the chapter "Having Bad Feelings Linger Less," which is why it is important for you to complete this section now.

Now we will deal with the pleasant or desired emotions, those we want to increase and have them linger longer. The process is the same as before, except the Value is "Yes." Use the same rating scales On pages 41- 42.

What To Do: Identify your least frequent and less intense desired emotions.

Why To Do It: You will be better prepared to analyze prompting events for wanted emotions.

**How To Do It: Place a check mark next to
the feelings with a Frequency of 1 or 2 _and_ an
Intensity of 1 or 2 _and_ are Valued as Yes.**

Examples:

Feelings	Situations That Make Me Feel That Way
Cheerful	- When my family compliments me on my meal
	- When I close a deal at work
	- When I finish a difficult task at home
	- When I help my son with his homework and he says at the end "That wasn't as hard as I thought it would be"
Enthusiastic	- When I'm planning the next family vacation
	- When I see on the news that someone did something heroic for their fellow man
	- When I get an assignment back from the professor and he writes what a wonderful job I did on the essay
Joy	- When I pet the dog and I see the appreciation in her eyes and her wagging tail
	- When I dress up my family and myself for church, and notice what a handsome family we are
	- When I get out of my procrastination rut and actually feel that I did something important

Mirth	-	When I'm around someone who tells jokes well
	-	-When someone says something clumsy and we all giggle at it
	-	When I'm able to giggle about my own buffoonery

Feelings	Situations That Make Me Feel That Way

We will return to this assignment in the next chapter "Having Wanted Feelings Linger Longer."

Threat Assessments

As mentioned, many of our perceptions are anticipatory. Bad things or feelings will happen if you don't do this or that. Also threats are perceived (most of our modern day threats are psychological rather than physical). A perceived threat may be actual or only feared to exist. For a school-aged child the threat may be bullying on the playground, or teased, or in the classroom that he will not receive the attention he seeks without acting out. For the adolescent the threat may be social nonacceptance from peers. For the adult the threat may be losing your job, having your spouse leave you, contracting a disease, or being lonely.

Some threats are real. You may be worried about losing your job only after you received two written warnings from your supervisor regarding your low productivity. Under this situation the threat job loss is real. But if you fret over losing your job only because Sally in another department was dismissed from employment then perhaps your sense of threat is misplaced.

Our attention to cues in the environment that predict threat are higher when we are highly anxious, and once threatened highly anxious people find it more difficult to disengage from the sense of threat (Johnstone & Walter, 2014). The same thing is true for many conditions where your emotions are high (depressed people focus on depressing threats like feelings of hopelessness, helplessness, and low worthiness, angry people focus on possible sources of attack from others, and social phobics focus on potential humiliation and social exposure).

Your ability to reasonably re-asses threat, especially when you are experiencing any feeling strongly, is thus wise.

**What To Do: Assess the frequency of
things you find threatening.**

**Why To Do It: Invites you to think about your concerns.
Prepares you for the following exercises
where you reassess them.**

**How To Do It: Read the list below, and make a forced
choice between never (it is not something you are aware
of), sometimes (it pops in and out of your head now
and then), or often (you are concerned with it a lot).**

Threat Situation	Never	Sometimes	Often
Intruder entering house			
Embarrassed in public			
Being taken advantage of			
Losing friends			
Losing an argument			
Looking stupid			
Having a life threatening illness or disease			
Being told harshly that I'm wrong			
Loss of my job			
Loss of my marriage			
My children dying before I do			
Having a panic attack in public			
Making a fool of myself in public			
Not locking the doors at night before bedtime			
Having my tax returns audited by the IRS			
Losing the respect of my loved ones			
Being falsely accused of wrongdoing			
Crying uncontrollably			

Going crazy			
Being caught cheating on a test	___	___	___
Commit adultery	___	___	___
Having my partner commit adultery	___	___	___
Having strangers unexpectedly knock on the door	___	___	___
Being seen in the nude	___	___	___
Blundering at a game	___	___	___
Being noticed by others	___	___	___
Not being noticed by others	___	___	___
Losing face	___	___	___
Being told that what I just said was illogical, and then being told how that was so	___	___	___
Having the wrong feeling	___	___	___
Not being able to stop feelings I have	___	___	___
Feeling ugly	___	___	___
Using a public restroom	___	___	___
Feeling unacceptable	___	___	___
Being threatened because of my race	___	___	___
Going to a public event and fear of being shot by terrorists	___	___	___
Tampering with food	___	___	___
Other:	___	___	___
Other:	___	___	___
Other:	___	___	___

Most of these threats are real. People do get shot by terrorists, robberies do occur, people are publicly shamed, racism does exist planetwide, murder occurs, and divorce does occur. In the next exercise you are asked not to deny the existence of the threats you worry about (many of which are real), but looking above at your checks you can see some are low frequency and some are high. Look at how the high frequency threats alter your behavior and alter your feelings. Make a plan on how to better deal with the real threats you feel.

What To Do: Reappraise threat cues.

Why To Do It: Threats limit your freedom, constrain your behavior and heightens your feelings. Having a plan to minimize threat perception can help you regain freedoms lost.

How To Do It: Choose three "Often" threats from above (the ones you feel most strongly about). Write a plan to minimize the effect of the threat and increase your confidence in the behaviors you engage in to deal with the real feelings you have.

Example:

Threat	Plan To Deal With The Threat
Being threatened because of my race	- I'll wear a shirt that reads "Make America Love Again" - Learn more about my cultural history and demographics to develop pride - Not use a a racial filter myself (like bigots do) to view all negative in my life - Not let racial issues interfere with my daily ability to enjoy life (walk away from racial situations rather than avoid going out in public)

Threat	Plan To Deal With The Threat
_____	_____
_____	_____
_____	_____
_____	_____
_____	_____
_____	_____
_____	_____
_____	_____
_____	_____
_____	_____
_____	_____
_____	_____
_____	_____
_____	_____
_____	_____

If you find yourself frequently afraid, anxious, tense, or distressed something is prompting it. Feelings come for a reason; there is a source. Identify the source.

In this chapter we have identified a number of components or factors that prompt feelings:

Feeling Factor or Component	How It Affects Us
Body	Relaxed muscles predict good feelings. Tight muscles predict bad feelings. Tight muscles prompt a sense of threat.
Thoughts	Positive thoughts predict good feelings. Negative thoughts predict distress, anguish, annoyance, anger or other unwanted feelings.
Genetics	Some people are biologically "hard-wired" to experience life with either low or high intensity. By definition that which is hard-wired can't be changed. But accepting your genetic predisposition (recognizing it and taking it in to account in your daily coping) is exceptionally helpful. People with low intensity need to "amp up" their expressiveness in interpersonal situations, while those with high intensity need to "tone down" their demonstrativeness. The same with internal experiences (coping with self).
Social	Society has social expectations, these vary by time and culture, but generally they are pretty steady. If you abide by social standards you are rewarded. If you disobey social standards you are punished. (Even in private internal experiences we do the same: reward or punish ourselves for compliance or disobedience.)

Values and Meanings	What a situation means to you determines the intensity of your feelings. When you behave consistent with your values (being monogamous in a marriage) then you feel badly when you lust for those outside your relationship.
Situations and Events	Frequently our feelings are prompted by things coming from the environment. Sometimes the feeling is not immediate: the delay in feeling—until it "hits you"—can make it difficult at times to identify the situation.
Threat Appraisals	Threat cues are "schemas" through which we filter our experience. Although threat is often real, we can allow threat to unnecessarily decrease our joy in life.

HOW TO MAKE WANTED FEELINGS LINGER

Why don't feelings linger? I think the answer is biological and about survival. A feeling is both about attraction and escape. When the situation is pleasant (safe and desired), we have the biological imperative to approach or invite it. When the situation is dangerous, you need to avoid or flee from it. Why do I call these things biological? Because feelings are designed to provide *immediate* and *imperative* information about survival, procreation, and comfort. In historical cave man/cave woman times you may not have had time to *think* things through. So feelings don't linger since they are designed, biologically, to provide immediate, short-term reactions to situations that confront you. Feelings need to "reset" so that when new and different situations occur, a new and different imperative (feeling) is ready to be noticed. Feelings do not naturally linger. In modern society, if we want certain feelings to linger we have to *make them* do so.

The question becomes when you desire to have a certain feeling, or set of feelings, linger, how do you do so? Since feelings are *provoked* (caused) by environmental or situational factors, in order to reproduce, rekindle, or reignite a feeling, you have to manipulate the environment. The word manipulate has a bad rap. Many think of it as a bad thing, like trying to get someone to do something they don't want to do. But think about it, we constantly manipulate the environment if we are successful at life. We manipulate food products and equipment in the kitchen to prepare a meal. More simply, we manipulate the credit card or cash out of our billfold or purse to purchase a meal. We manipulate the phone to make to make a phone call. We manipulate a big social occasion (like a wedding) by sending out invitations. We manipulate our children by telling them playtime is over and it is time for bed. We manipulate our friends to come over by asking them to do so. Manipulation is not a bad thing, instead it is strategically influencing the environment for a desired outcome.

People tend to resent having to influence their environment to change their feelings. Look at Table 4 below. They are all ways of complaining about taking responsibility for our feelings. If this sounds sharp and disapproving, it is not meant to be. Instead, it is reality that effectiveness as a person requires that we, too, have to influence our environment in order to reproduce (or simply produce) the feelings we want to have. Other people (our children, our friends, our neighbors, our spouses) do it all the time. So can you.

Values	Negative Thoughts, Attitudes, or Doubts
Honesty	True honesty is unobtainable.
Integrity	You miss important opportunities because your ethics tell you what should or should not be done.
Compassion	Caring about others does little to help them.

Empathy	Understanding others does little to help them. You should help them solve problems so there will be no need for empathy.
Love	You may get hurt, so why bother?
Courage	Let the other guy get it instead of me.
Friendship	You are safer if you trust no one. You're taking a risk.
Peace of mind (security, safety)	It's only an illusion. There is always danger.
Life	You're going to die anyway.
Choice, freedom	Another illusion. In the end, nothing matters.
Companionship	Safety is more important than being with someone. They can always let you down.
Pets	They poop all over the place and destroy things you like.
Family	They will all die at some time, so why attach to them so strongly?
Community	Every community is the same. One is the same as another.
Recreation	It will all end. It's only a temporary diversion from ultimate pain.
Creativity	There will always be a critic. You can't please them all. It doesn't last.
Art	Most people never succeed in the arts, and what does success bring you?
Beauty	Age destroys it. It's temporary. It's up to the beholder (so it's not universal and therefore ultimately unimportant).
Nature	Transitory and difficult to maintain while caring for self. Another delusional value.
Earth	Ultimately not under our control, and why worry about that which cannot be controlled?

Imagination	Just another way of avoiding reality.
Memories	Living in the past doesn't help now or in the future.
Eternal life	Our meager existence is already too long.
Spirituality	We are on our own. Avoiding reality with delusion ultimately leads to disappointment.
Energy	Unnecessary movement.
Purpose	What real important purpose is there? We live, then we die.
Familiarity	Needed by small minds.
Predictability	Brings routine, ruts, and allows people to second-guess you.
Trustworthiness	A fool's delight. You end up getting in trouble anyway.
Loyalty	Falling off the cliff with your buddies is no better than falling off alone.
Justice	All relative. One man's justice is another's punishment.
Acceptance	Another concept for small minds, designed to deny the true futility of existence.
Discovery	We know all that is needed to know. Trying to find out more is just a waste of time.
Awareness	Knowing the bogeyman is going to get you doesn't bring comfort.
Desire to learn and seek knowledge	Catching up with others who are also doomed is no accomplishment
Being understood	Having people agree with us that things are bad is little consolation.
Self-esteem	Feeling good about being inadequate gets us nowhere.
Success	There will always be someone better who has more and got it more easily.

Accomplishment	Another self-delusion.
Contributions to others	They are not grateful, and they take it for granted. It gets the collective "us" little.
Truth	It's all relative.
Stimulation	Masturbation. A temporary comfort not ultimately important.
Sensitivity	It just opens you up to hurt. Why be a sucker?
Morals, ethics	The meek will inherit the earth. But only after the rest have spoiled it.
Courtesy	Meant for weaklings who can't defend themselves and are trying to not make enemies.

Table 4: Values And How We Can Argue Ourselves Out of Them

As the Table above shows, you can always criticize values, find competing perspectives, and find reasons to believe in nothing. What is useful in terms of making feelings linger is to temporarily suspend your judgmentalism and sustain mindfulness to the positive emotion you feel. Return later and make something previously unimportant important. Anxiety makes you doubt, to fear what you want because you may not get it. Doubt is antithetical to mindfulness and creating and sustaining wanted feelings. It seems to be easier for many people to lose meaning than it is to create it.

WORDS

Words can be murky waters to swim in, but I want to define a few to guide you through the next sections.

Inspiration (Oxford English Dictionary, Vol. VII, 2001):

Literal physical senses...The action of blowing on or into...The action or an act, of breaching in...or infusion into the mind or soul...A special immediate action or influence of the Spirit of God. A breathing in or infusion of some idea, purpose, etc. into the mind; the suggestion, awakening, or creation of some feeling or impulse, esp. of an exalted kind (page 1036).

Meaning (Oxford English Dictionary, Vol. IX. 2001):

Intention, purpose...Strong inclination...That which is intended to be...Significance, knowledge, understanding...Having a recognizable purpose or function (page 522).

Vivid (Oxford English Dictionary, Vol. XIX, 2001):

Full of life; vigorous, active, or energetic...Strongly or warmly expressed... Capable of ready and clear creation of ideas or concepts...presenting subjects or ideas in a clear and striking manner...of colour, light, etc.: brilliant, fresh, lively, bright...clearly or distinctly perceived or perceptible; appealing strongly to the mind or eye...Intensely or strongly felt...life-like, resembling life (page 715).

So, as you practice the following exercises, try to deploy all three abilities: Be inspired (don't wait for God, just infuse it into your mind and soul), do it meaningfully (do it with purpose and intention), and make it vivid (active, clear, lively, bright, and strongly felt).

Go back to the exercise on pages 45 – 47 where the Value was "Yes" and you wrote the wanted feelings in one column and the situations that create them in the next. Repeat those experiences, those prompting events for the pleasant feelings, as often as you can, while being mindful to the situation *and* to the simultaneous feelings.

Shift your attention back and forth between the experience and your feelings. This heightens the feeling

---

What To Do: Choose several events you find pleasant and repeat them. Repeat them often, not all at once, but throughout the day periodically.

Why To Do It: The best way to have wanted feelings stick around is to have plans and action for frequent prompting events Journaling your experiences helps you re-member with them.

How To Do It: Journal your experiences in the chart below. Write what you did in the first column, how it felt in the second column

---

Examples:

What I Did	How I Felt
I talked to a good friend on the phone for over 30 minutes. We discussed so many things!	*Happy*

I closed a big business deal. My supervisor was pleased. It is going to bring in lots of money to the company. I may get a raise or promotion.   *Satisfaction*

I finished my history essay for school. I re-read it, and I think it is very well written.   *Relief; Good about myself*

Do the same as in the examples. But place the general date so you know how frequently you are creating wanted feelings.

Date	What I Did	How I Felt

Journaling is exceptionally important. Do this exercise routinely, at least for a few months, to ignite your enthusiasm and make it a habit in your life. A blank form is provided in the back of this book in the appendices. Photocopy those forms while they are blank so you can use them again and again.

Difficulty: What if you don't have enough events that make you feel good feelings? Explore the world more fully and all the possibilities available to you.

Guidelines for Increasing Positive Emotional Experiences

1. Pay attention to the activity. Be mindful. Watch each element of what is going on like you have never experienced it before.
2. Be engaged. Actively participate. Let other thoughts and ideas that are not related to what you are doing fade away. Focus your energy and concentration on the enjoyable moment
3. Pay attention to the now. Don't think about when it will end or how long it will last.
4. Pay attention to the feelings in the moment. Don't compare them to previous feelings, anticipated feelings, or ideas about how others might feel when they are engaged in the activity.

5. Don't wait for a particular level of satisfaction or enjoyment to appear before you further engage in the activity. Be mindful of the now.

Behavioral Activation and Novelty

Positive experiences prompt and help create good feelings. Good feelings are a result of (in part) your reaction to situations, events, and experiences. So why don't we frequently engage in situations that prompt good feelings? There are beliefs that prevent engagement in positive experiences.

Beliefs That Prevent Engagement in Positive Experiences

"Why should I do anything? I'll just feel bad again afterward."

"I've tried doing stuff I use to like. It just doesn't feel the same as it used to."

"I can't think of anything fun to do."

"I don't have the energy. I would just be going through the motions, and that's no fun."

The following pages might prompt you to notice things that have already happened, that you fail to be mindful of, that could bring amusement if you let them. Notice that some of the ideas ask you to challenge *how* you do things (for example, doing what you've done before in the opposite direction or for the reverse purpose) so that you increase novelty.

- Play scrabble
- Dress up in your best clothes
- Give donations to your favorite charities
- Call someone about a game you just watched on TV
- Make a new friend
- Write a positive review of a product you bought over the internet
- Go to a concert
- Reminisce about the good times in your life
- Play solitaire

- Plan a cruise to an exotic place, even if you know you won't take it
- Go shopping
- Watch a nature show
- Say the Rosary
- Read some of the Bible
- Call some of your old military buddies
- Look at redecorating ideas
- Take a bubble bath
- Watch sports
- Plan some remodeling work
- Go to a horse show
- Try writing a poem
- Try a new restaurant
- Listen to a npr program you've never heard before
- Take a drive somewhere you've never been before
- Take a drive somewhere that previously had pleasant memories
- Take deep breaths and appreciate the rhythm of your breathing
- Listen to your favorite music
- Go to a bar and order a drink you've never had
- Make a banana or strawberry drink at home
- Pretend you're doing a news commentary and expressing your views
- Go on a sail boat
- Do something your parents asked you to do
- If typically you eat at drive-ins, dine in
- Go to a garage sale
- Rearrange your furniture
- Spray your house with your favorite air freshening scent
- Light a candle in the dark
- Think of arguments both for and against your own political views
- Get out an old photograph album and remember the good times
- Play a board game
- Think of something funny
- Go to a lake or stream
- Try your hand at artwork of any kind
- Laugh or think of something amusing
- Call a friend and set a date to get together
- Use of your time off days and practice relaxation
- Keep previously scheduled social events
- Use mouthwash mindfully
- Go running
- Walk the dog
- Write a short story
- Pet your dog or cat
- Take a hike
- Call a friend you have not talked to in ages
- Sing to yourself
- Make a list of all your positive attributes and qualities about which you are proud
- Think about how skillful you are at your work
- Give a party
- Go to church
- Go to a carnival and watch young kids on their rides
- Strike up a conversation or compliment a stranger
- Sing out loud
- Pray out loud
- Read a travel magazine
- If you live in a city, go to the country, if you live in the country go to a city
- Volunteer for a nonprofit
- If you are frequently on the internet, shift to magazines or books
- If you always read books, shift to the internet
- Go car shopping and sit in a fancy sport or luxury car
- Make surprise hors d'oeuvres for a friend or relative
- Be helpful to someone
- Wear your pajamas all day long

- Restyle your hair in the mirror
- Plan your costume for Halloween
- Watch a comedy
- If you're an exceptionally social person, spend one day entertaining yourself alone
- Make a recipe you've never tried before
- Drive on the scenic route, mindful of what you normally don't see
- Write a cost/benefit analysis of various approaches to solving a problem, and sit on the solutions for a day
- Make something (food, craft, furniture, art) to give away
- Plan a game to play with your grandchildren
- Go to a craft store and explore hobbies you have not done
- If you are a guy, put on makeup for fun
- Draw a diagram of your dream house (even if you know you'll never use it)
- Go to a nursing home and visit with people you don't know
- Go to a high school athletic game and practice cheerleading from the stands

- Think of a product that, if made, could make you millions
- Imagine being a movie star
- Rake leaves in your yard and feel satisfied
- Read about your high school or college on the internet
- Pretend you are a landscape architect and design the perfect yard
- Go dancing and be aware of how movement makes your body feel
- Let the sun hit your face, and feel the warmth
- Look up at the clouds and see if you can imagine shapes in them
- Look up at the stars, and feel
- Think of something ridiculous, like how you would explain the human condition to an alien from another planet
- Go to an elegant hotel in your best clothes and go to their cocktail lounge
- Image good things happening to your family and friends
- Go to a zoo and watch animal behavior intently

- Go to a lecture on philosophy or religion
- Go to a casino and watch other people gamble someone
- Listen to birds chirp and sing
- Flirt with someone
- If you are a talker, practice being a listener
- If you are a listener, practice being a talker
- Play a competitive game
- Listen to a radio station you've not heard before
- Invite people over and don't clean the place beforehand
- Think about how to make a new friend
- Plan a gift for a friend
- Take a community college course on a topic unfamiliar to you
- Go to a spa
- Write a "thinking of you" card to a distant friend
- Listen to the sound of rain
- Plan a picnic
- Watch travel shows
- Stretch your muscles, and then mindfully feel the difference in them
- Think of the best joke you've ever heard
- Try to create a new joke
- Go to an art exhibit
- Go to a museum
- Travel to a state you've never been

- Buy a fresh bouquet of flowers
- Clean your desk of clutter
- When doing a chore you don't like, practice mindfulness of body and try to stay out of your head
- Attend a lecture or poetry reading
- Go to a new coffee and tea shop
- Eat a good meal mindfully
- Turn off the TV for an entire day
- Write a speech, even if you'll never deliver it
- Organize your closet or store room, then look at the finished product and feel good about your efforts
- Give yourself time to feel
- Give yourself time to think
- Think about things you do on "auto pilot" and do them mindfully
- Compliment yourself when you've done a job well
- Go fishing, not to catch fish but to relax and change pace
- Allocate spare time to do something productive rather than fun
- Think about ways to balance spiritual,
- productive, and relationship-building activites in your life
- Loan something small to someone when you know you'll never get it back
- Imagine yourself as sexy and romantic
- Do something to please both your superiors and subordinates
- Give someone good advice
- When someone remembers what you've said, remember to feel good (doesn't always happen)
- Do something you know you're not good at (scrabble, crossword puzzles, cards) to stretch your limits rather than win
- Practice the art of compliments: find the good rather than the bad in others
- Think more often about people you like or admire
- Join a book club (preferably in-person, but if you live in the country then by mail)
- Practice being nice to people who are mean to you
- Spend more or less time with family; change routine
- Imagine yourself doing something you would never do (skydiving, mountain climbing, boxing, playing in the mud
- Find ways to advocate for the underserved
- Rather than talk on the telephone to a distant friend, write them a letter
- Allow yourself to daydream
- Act like a kid (kick leaves, engage in unnecessary movements, skip pebbles on the water)
- Think like a kid (do I have to, not again, you can't make me), then grow up
- Kiss your spouse the way you did in the beginning
- Analyze your own dreams
- Sleep in late, or get up early
- Allow both alone and social time
- Allow peace and quiet time (no TV, radio, music, phone; and watch where your mind goes)
- When someone needs you, see that as a gift rather than a burden
- Coach little league, or take your children to a game
- Go to a nursery

- Think of those with challenges (poverty, blindness, missing body parts, hunger, lack of water, people who live in war zones) and count your blessings
- When watching the news, reading a newspaper or the internet, give thanks for a free press
- Remember the olden days when almost all time was spent finding food and shelter, and give thanks for what you have
- If you are competitive at games, remember fun can be had even when you lose
- When having sex, focus on making love rather than the orgasm
- Spend time with happy people, and cherish them
- People are fascinating. When in a group of strangers (mall, shopping center, restaurant), engage in people watching
- Build a fire and watch the flames in the breeze
- When presenting an opposing argument to someone, don't try to get them to agree (you'll enjoy it more)
- Cook meals with spices, and smell them prior to putting them in to the mixture
- Confess or apologize, and feel good about yourself as a strong rather than defensive person
- When you budget your time, try not to feel urgency but preparedness
- Give yourself a break; be less judgmental of any faults (everyone has them)
- Be sensual with everyday chores (washing your body and hair, feeding the dog, washing the dishes, etc.)
- Listen to criticism without feeling bad
- Make certain your ratio of giving criticism is vastly outweighed by your compliments
- Feel pride for others when others succeed
- Smile often (even when alone)
- Spend quality time with those you love
- Walk barefoot in a stream, lake, or ocean
- Be aware of multitasking. Efficiency sometimes is not as important as feeling
- If you are not typically a cook, bake a cake
- Try to impress people
- Stop trying to impress people
- Give your friends the attention they deserve.
- Watch attractive women or men with appreciation rather than envy
- Go to a forest or beach and experience nature
- Bicycle while feeling the air on your face
- Practice loving when you are with someone you love
- When someone shows interest in what you said or what you've done, enjoy it
- Read humor (comics, jokes, or have your children tell you something funny that happened at school or in a cartoon)
- Watch children play (on TV, at the park, at your own home)
- Imagine yourself the Queen of England, and bite your tongue when someone does something distasteful
- Watch some Netflix
- Let somebody coach you
- Think of your favorite teachers
- Plan a camping trip.
- Dance alone, or with others
- Go to live theatre.
- Stop yourself from getting on the internet

Expanding Positive Experiences

Having feelings linger longer is about the frequency you prompt those feelings through experience. You've identified experiences from the past that make you feel good, and journaling those feelings make you remember and appreciate them again (reigniting the good feeling). *Expanding* the different kinds of experiences that can bring wanted feelings is an excellent way to increase happiness. In the next exercise choose five experiences you do very infrequently (or not at all) and try them over the next week. Record how you felt and how likely you are to repeat them, as well as any "costs" associated with them. (A cost could be it takes too much time, costs too much money, irritates someone you care about, interrupts your desired routines, or is inconsistent with how you see yourself.) For example, in the last example if your mother is a realtor and you know she is upset when people take a large amount of her time and never buy a house, you may choose not to go house hunting because you are not in the market for one, although you feel good doing so.)

Remember to be mindful of the experience when you engage in it. Mindfulness of the event, mindful of your feelings, and going back and forth between self and environment.

What To Do: Pick an activity you do infrequently or never, that may be appealing.

Why To Do It: It will expand your menu of fun, enjoyment, and amusement.

How To Do It: Chose an activity, engage in it mindfully, reflect on it thinking of positives first and negatives last. Journal your responses below.

Never or Rarely Did	What I Felt	Costs
Swimming. I'm not afraid of the water, but just had not done it since a kid. Found a heated community pool.	Didn't really try to swim, but enjoyed the warm water, the sense of buoyancy of my body, Felt fluid, sensual on my skin.	Bit self-conscious of being in a bathing suit, but everyone was attending to their own experience and not me.
Discussed politics with my friend. Have been told never talk about politics, religion, or money.	I was surprised how much people attend to national politics, how engaging our conversation was, and it felt really good to talk about something besides family and work like I do most of the time.	Afraid I didn't know enough to speak intelligently, that my views might offend someone because their views were stronger than mine.
Played a video game. My kids do it constantly (that concerns me) so had them show me how to play with them.	Enjoyed spending time with my son, shared his joy that I showed interest in his passion, felt closer to him and had fun.	Of course lost the game, felt inadequate that I could not control the buttons fast enough (what happened to my dexterity?) Judgmental that it was a waste of time that my son spends so much time on these games.

Never or Rarely Did	How I Felt	Costs

In the next example you are asked to reappraise the "costs" from the previous exercise. You can only do this after you have completed the previous exercise. Examine your costs above, and challenge those notions.

**What To Do: Look at your "costs" above.
Challenge their basis, value, or effect.**

**Why To Do It: Gain perspective, free
yourself from needless constraints.**

**How To Do It: Abbreviate the event in the first column.
Abbreviate the costs in the second column. Look at
the last column from the above exercise. In the third
column develop contradictory reasons, evidence, or
experience to counter what you initially reported.**

Example:

Event	Costs	Reappraisal

Swimming	Self-conscious	Who cares what they think! I'm not there to show off my body, or to model swim wear, I'm there to enjoy myself, to experience good feelings. No one paid attention to me anyway. It was wasted concern that decreased my enjoyment a little bit.
Politics	Fear not informed, inadequacy, offend someone	Lots of people talk about things they are ill informed about, And it is not like I don't watch the news. I'm not an expert, but my lay opinion is worth as much as another lay person's is. I'm too hard on myself. If I offend someone because my views are different than yours then maybe it is that they are judgmental. This is a democracy, and reasonable people disagree.
Video Game	Lost, dexterity, judgmentalism	I don't need to play a game to win. My son has lots and lots of practice and I don't. It would have been worse for him had I won on my first try and he lost for that reason. I played the game for two reasons: do something different and share a new experience with my son. I accomplished both. And my dexterity is fine for the tasks I perform daily.

Event	Costs	Reappraisal

Rekindling Prompts

Emotions that we like can also be prompted with previous prompts: a photograph album from family events, reading letters you saved from others, watching home movies your family made, visiting the home where you grew up, going in to the attic or garage and looking at things from the past, going in to your closet and remembering when you first wore that suit or dress for a special occasion, looking at the old set of baseball cards you collected as a child, or visiting a recreational area or park to which your family went. Choose something special, magical, and pleasant.

Re-membering Prompts

I place a hyphen on remembering on purpose: to member again with an experience and the feeling with which it is attached. Memory itself can ignite feelings. Remember your first day at school, your high school graduation, your wedding day, the birth of your first child, when you first learned to ride a bicycle, your very first paycheck, when you first learned to tie your own shoe laces, your first date, your college days, when your parents first joyfully exclaimed that you can read, or when you started your first business. The specific topic does not matter, rather it is the pleasant experiences with which it is associated.

Vicarious Prompts

We learn and feel from others. It is not *our* experience, but through empathy and compassion we feel what he or she did. When you watch a news or documentary about the heroic or simply successful defeat against all odds you feel compelled to happily cry in joy, you get goose bumps, or you feel emboldened and share in their delight, exult in their contentment. Vicarious prompts can be movies, television, a neighbor's story, the newspaper, the radio, or even music as you listen to the lyrics and the passion from the singer.

If you feel there are not elements from your own past that prompt joy and happiness, think about the joy and pleasure others have experienced.

Engage in these experiences to increase and make good feelings linger.

What To Do: Chose an experience from each category above (rekindling, re-membering, and vicarious) and engage in it.

Why To Do It: It provides "remote" pleasure not necessarily dependent on others. It is something you can do frequently to make good feelings linger.

How to Do It: With inspiration, meaning, and vividness, complete this exercise of feeling good.

Example:

Type of Experience	Object	What I Did	How it Made Me Feel
Rekindle	baseball cards	I looked at them and remembered how mom said it was a waste of money but let me do it anyway, how dad supported me, and how much glee I received from my classmates when we compared and shared	Glee, nostalgic, happy, pleasant
Re-member	First paycheck	I remember I thought I was rich! It was only $350	Amazement, amusement, and silliness that I was so immature

Vicarious	Movie: "A Dogs Purpose"	Watched the movie mindfully	Felt all kinds of things, sadness, anger, but at end was crying with joy (feel tearful joy right now writing about it)

Type of Experience	Object	What I Did	How it Made Me Feel
Rekindle			
Re-member			
Vicarious			

Reappraisal

In the previous exercises you were invited to welcome new and different experiences in to your life. Novelty can be a powerful reinforcer (gets us out of ruts, routines, habits, and rumination that occur during repetitive behavior). In this exercise we will explore issues that prevent us from engaging in new or novel behavior.

Happiness can be prevented or interrupted because we have false conceptions about our world (Ryan & Deci, 2001). Here "false" does not mean lack of reality testing, it means not necessarily true. It may be true for you because you have not tested it out for you. Some of our conceptions are tested without awareness. Our mother says "hot" and we touch it anyway. We learn it is hot. Some of our conceptions are tested consciously. You may say to yourself "I'll never get that job" but apply because your spouse or parents pressure you to do so, and you get the job. We all have preconceived notions about our world, but the principal of reappraisal asks us to challenge these notions, to test them out.

Reappraisal is thus when you ask yourself questions: Is this belief true (and to what degree), or am I correct in my assumptions? Moreover, reappraisal asks us to examine the interplay of thoughts and feelings (McKay, 2011). Sometimes our beliefs (a thought) are based on feelings. At other times our feelings are based on thoughts. Reappraisal is thus requesting that you "ask yourself," "challenge," or "reexamine" your appraisal or conception.

Self-Compassion

The Oxford English Dictionary (2001) defines compassion as suffering together, fellow-feeling, sympathy, when a person is moved by the suffering or distress of another (and by the desire to relieve it), to spare or to succor, and be sympathetic. Succor is to help or relieve, helpful, and giving assistance. Self-Compassion would be the same process, giving sympathetic succorance to self. Fellow-feeling, being empathic and compassionate to yourself is most likely practicing the very emotion we give to others to ourselves. I would posit that it impairs one's ability to give to others when one does not give to one's self. And studies have shown the benefits of self-compassion and self-support (Hoffman, Grossman, & Hinton, 2011).

Think about the concept of fellow-feeling. It is empathy; I can feel what you feel. Perhaps you can't feel exactly what another feels because you are not them, you can feel closely, with either joy or suffering—you share the emotional experience with them. Fellow-feeling is thus "oneness" with them. Self-compassion is thus similar, becoming one with yourself, providing succor to yourself.

Self-compassion is about thankfulness for what you are rather than what you are not, about excavating and appreciating what your sense of self is (explored more fully in another chapter) rather than what it is not. It is not exactly about forgiveness (because that comes after identifying deficiencies), but rather about positive affirmation of your strengths, qualities, and feelings that you value.

Self-support can be distinguished from comparative statements about others. Comparison may be ego enhancing, but at the expense of others (which is not fellow-feeling). Simple examples would be:

Self-Support	Comparative Support
I am a good person.	I'm a better person than Keith.
I love myself.	I certainly do more good in the world than Mary.
I can take care of myself. I'm competent.	I do a better job at living my life than my family ever did.

Self-compassion serves several purposes: it enhances one's self-esteem, it provides emotional energy and enthusiasm, it focuses on support rather than criticism, it employs self-talk to direct our attention to self, and it serves as a contemplative form of meditation that is soothing and self-supporting. It can thus make positive feelings linger longer.

Engaging in self-support should be both independent of negative life events (practiced routinely for preventative purposes, to inoculate yourself against undesired events and environments in the future), as well as retrospectively (after a negative event that challenges your self-esteem or confidence). Such affirmations of self are resisted by many as being egotistical or silly. Self-compassion is not egotistical. Here are some examples of egotistical statements:

- I'm the best damn carpenter in this state.
- I can challenge anyone to a debate and win.
- My pies have won more awards in the state fair than anyone else has.

Notice any themes in these egotistical statements? They are comparative. How about being silly? Look at these statements:

- My body is so in shape, I could be Atlas and hold up the world!
- My fingers are so nimble, I can probably keyboard 10,000 words per minute.
- I don't need to study; I know everything already.

Self-compassion is not egotistical or silly. It is supportive and self-enhancing (not at the expense of others and not over inflated). Importantly, it is a private experience. You do not engage in self-compassion in discourse with another person (to impress them, negotiate with them, or put them down). Self-compassion is what you say to yourself, in your thoughts, and not out loud to others.

Is the following exercise designed to develop pride? Yes, it is. While pride is described as one of the seven deadly sins, that is because it is applied inappropriately and misunderstood (Tracy, 2016).

Self-compassion can be difficult prophylactically (when you are being self-supporting without forgiveness). Why? How do you prepare yourself for something you are not expecting or anticipating?

What can I say about myself that is not egotistical or silly? How many times can I say that I love myself without **me** feeling silly?

Here are some suggestions, but it is more important that you develop your own:

- I know I'm a good person.
- I do my best not to hurt others.
- I respect my fellow man.
- I am a moral person; I think about what I do and how it may affect others.
- I work hard for my goals.
- I correct my mistakes.
- I think about the planet on which I live, and attempt to protect it.
- I am a kind person.
- I have flexible standards. I'm not rigid in my thinking.
- I give more than I receive, and don't resent it.
- I share what I have.
- I hold hands, and feel the bond between me and others.
- I feel part of a community.
- I am thankful.
- I appreciate my feelings.

I understand that this task is ambiguous, but please engage in self-compassion for at least one minute each morning, before you begin your day. See it as a way of providing yourself grace from yourself and from the universe in which you live.

What To Do: Develop scripts that you can say to yourself each morning.

Why To Do It: Help positive feelings
linger, develop higher self-esteem.

How To Do It: Identify what you are proud of, why
you are proud of it, and take notes so you don't forget.
Practice it daily for one minute, in your head.

Notes on My Self-Compassion Statements

```
_____
_____
_____
_____
_____
_____
```

Having positive feelings linger thus involves: identifying the feelings you want to increase (naming them and experiencing them mindfully), having inspiration (physical sensations and energy), having meaning (a sense of purpose), having them be vivid (creating vigorous and energizing clarity), practicing activities that feel good, expanding the menu of activities that make you feel good, reappraising thoughts that inhibit feeling good, and engaging in self-compassion.

If you are saying to yourself "I did all those exercises and still don't feel happier," perhaps it is because you are at the beginning of your journey to have good feelings linger. You would not want a neurosurgeon to operate on your brain, no matter how badly you needed such surgery, if she had only done it once before. You would want her to have lots of experience, with many patients over a period of years.

At the back of the workbook are blank forms for you to photocopy while blank. Use them routinely to both practice these skillsets and to journal your experiences.

All of these elements involve steady practice, growing the wanted feelings in what can become habits of daily life. With practice you get better at it. Emotion regulation is a set of skills that have to be practiced in order to be effective.

So in this chapter we have reviewed the broad topics below to have positive feelings linger:

- Name the feeling
- Use mindfulness to "engage" with the feeling
- Find new things to expand positive emotional experiences
- Identify obstacles and overcome them
- Rekindle and use memories for more positive feelings
- Use vicarious prompts to have more positive feelings
- Engage in self-compassion
- Increase the frequency of prompts for feeling good, and practice them regularly.

HOW TO HAVE UNWANTED FEELINGS FADE

Techniques and strategies to deal with unpleasant feelings are many. Some use denial, but that is an ineffective process. Some use avoidance, and that is a much more useful process but frequently unsustainable. Changing your perspective (your thoughts) is good, if this is realistic in your situation. Using the biopsychosocial model to intervene in any of the powering factors of your experience has been shown to have excellent results. Changing the prompting events is quite effective. Lastly, actually changing your environment can be sustainable and effective, if it is realistic. We will explore each of these alternatives in this chapter.

DENIAL

Denial is when you say something to yourself or others like: "I don't know what you are talking about. I didn't do that." "What, I'm to fault for this mess! What mess?" "I'm not upset. Why do you keep telling me to lower my voice?" "You are the problem…I've had no part in this." "My family is not dysfunctional. Why do you find fault with everything they do." "You are just too demanding. Grow up! I don't want to hear anymore from you." Perhaps the worst, "I don't care what you feel. End of discussion."

Simply put, denial is when you say this is not happening (when it is). Denial is when you point the finger at others and the focus is on blame, rather than mutuality (that we live in a social context and all play our part, consciously or unconsciously). Denial is the lack of recognition of experience itself. It is unmindful and not thoughtful. It does not work. In fact, it makes matters worse much of the time.

How do you know if you are in denial? By definition denial is not experiencing what is happening, so mindfulness and self-exploration can be helpful. The most effective strategy is to take in what is being said from others seriously. If your spouse says to you, "Honey you are getting drunk every night," rather than defend yourself, "You are a worry wart, it is not a problem for anyone but you," take in what they are saying, consider the feedback as a good piece of information to act on. People consume alcohol for a variety of reasons (to self-soothe, to avoid feeling what they are feeling, out of simple addiction, to try to bring conviviality in to their lives, etc.). Frequently drinking alone is a sign something else is going on (addiction or escape).

Another common experience of denial is around anger (that can be expressed through mean words to another, throwing things about the room, raised volume of voice, sarcasm, excessive criticism of another person without balancing it with support and affection, pouting, disobedience of rules, slow and rapid breathing, or even just feeling superior to others). The key factor here is that you *behave* with anger, but do not identify or experience the anger.

Insecurity is often an experience that people deny rather than cope with in more effective ways. Unfortunately, a frequent way to deny insecurity is to use what Freud (1905) called a reaction formation: you express superiority or hatred in extraordinary ways that belie your underlying insecurity. Examples might be telling people how smart you are, how you think when you read about geniuses in print that they are fools to think so highly of themselves, when you tell an expert in a certain field that they do not know what they are talking about, when you exaggerate your accomplishments in school—or just exaggerate about all your qualities, or simply communicate an air of "I know better than most others" or worse "I know better than all others." It can be subtle behavior you might engage in, like yawning and looking bored in class when you are denying feeling insecure about your learning potential or the grade you will receive.

Denial is thus a form of many defense mechanisms.

Here are some clues that may suggest denial:

- You've received the same or similar feedback from more than one person, and you still don't accept it
- You effortfully avoid people or situations that could provide you feedback, so you won't hear that feedback.
- When you see a behavior or characteristic in others that you strongly despise, perhaps it is because you have the tendency to that behavior or characteristic.
- When you get exceptionally angry or anxious when someone says it

In the next exercise, attempt to identify at least two areas in which you *may* be in denial. Think about the feedback you get from others. Denial is about looking deeper than your known feelings. So if you know you feel insecure because you *feel* it, then you are not in denial about it. Think about repetitive feedback you have received from others *that are about feelings or behavior expressing feelings.* Not included in this category are *judgments* you may have heard from others intended to hurt or belittle you (like, statements that you are a slob, a reject, unworthy of love, a slut, a degenerate, a piece of shit) or derogatory statements that don't feel like feedback, not potentially helpful pieces of information or observations.

Example:

BEHAVIOR That Might Express Some Feeling Not Felt	Possible Feelings
I lie around the house many days and do not get anything done. I decline invitations to social or family events. People tell me I'm becoming reclusive.	Depression Dysphoria Social Anxiety Insecurity

Another example:

BEHAVIOR That Might Express Some Feeling Not Felt	Possible Feelings
I don't think that I overeat. People tell me the reason I'm having to buy new clothes is that I'm gaining weight. People tell me I have gained 50 pounds in the last year. I think I just like to eat.	Loneliness Boredom Anxiety relief with comfort foods

What To Do: Think of feedback you have received from others that you either discounted or dismissed.

Why To Do It: Explore hidden feelings, blind spots, or avoidance patterns that may not be working for you.

How To Do It: Think of feedback you receive frequently that you do not act on. Best ones to choose are when you receive the feedback frequently from people you like, trust, or love.

BEHAVIOR That Might Express Some Feeling Not Felt	Possible Feelings

AVOIDANCE

Not placing yourself in a hurtful situation that is unlikely to change is very effective. Examples would be when you leave a physically abusive spouse to avoid violence. You quit your job because of sexual harassment. You don't answer the phone when you know the caller is angry and is going to yell at you. You decide not to visit aunt Agnes because she treats you like a slave and shows no appreciation. You turn off the TV when you see emotionally provocative material (blood and gore, unnecessary evil being committed by a perpetuator, or redundant arguments). When you anticipate further unwanted emotions, preventing them from happening is efficacious.

The only problem (and this is a big one) with avoidance is that frequently we cannot, or do not, avoid the problematic situation. If your child tells you that you are a horrible parent, of course that hurts. Most parents don't put their child up for adoption, or evict them from the house, because they hurt them. If your spouse drinks too much alcohol at a social occasion and makes an embarrassment to you, most people do not immediately file for divorce. If your best friend flakes on you at the last minute because "something better came along" your first reaction may be to withdraw from the friendship. Emotional struggle is part of any close and ongoing relationship (family, job, friendships, and communities).

We will deal much more thoroughly with context (the roles you play in life, and their meaningfulness to you) in the next chapter. For now, just ask yourself these basic questions:

- How important is this person to you?
- How much would you miss this situation if it were lost?
- Is a substitute for this relationship or situation easily obtainable?
- Is the situation you're thinking of avoiding really the full cause of your pain?
- Is this just "the straw that broke the camel's back" or is it the exclusive reason for your feelings?

First, let's deal with situations where you believe it was the right thing to avoid, because the situation was painful, there was little hope of it ever changing, or it was dangerous to you. So you avoided the situation to improve your life.

Example:

In the following example you became obsessed with porn. You work at home. Your wife goes to her job. You are full of lust. You don't know why (you love your wife and feel she is beautiful and sexy). It got to the point you were not getting your work done, the income was not flowing in for the household, and the organizations that employ you were annoyed with your lower productivity. Perhaps worst of all, your wife starts to look at the history bar on your computer, and sees all the sex sites you have visited, day after day. She accuses you of not loving her, not being attracted to her, and says to you if you keep it up she is going to divorce you.

Situation/Feeling You Avoided	Resulting Situation/Feelings
The situation is pornography sites on the computer. The feeling is lust. Maybe if I see just one or two more nude women having sex with men this obsession will go away. But it never does. I commit to avoid porn sites forever.	Wife does not divorce me. Wife still loves me, and I love her. I make more money for us. The people I do work for are happier. There is less conflict inside of me and less conflict between my wife and I.

What To Do: Think of situations and feelings
you have skillfully avoided, where there
was a desired and wanted outcome.

Why To Do It: Understand that avoidance can be an appropriate
strategy. Enduring unnecessary pain and agony is hurtful.
Understanding that acting on urges is not always helpful.

How To Do It: Focus on successful avoidance
behavior. How did you do it?
What made it difficult to do? What got you through it?
What were the positive outcomes *and* feelings?

Situation/Feeling You Avoided	Resulting Situation/Feelings

Now let's deal with situations and feelings were avoidance does not work for you. Typically avoidance is used to avert negative feelings without notice or care about the intended outcomes of such avoidance. An example would be to not experience anxiety by remaining in the house if you are agoraphobic. The consequence is that you essentially are trapped in your own house or apartment, which can be dismal in a long-term way, but the short-term gain is not experiencing anxiety in the here-and-now. And this example gets at one of the primary core issues with avoidance: you sacrifice long-term goals in order to serve short-term objectives.

Another example would be your commitment to monogamy in your marriage. Sure, after 20 years in your marriage maybe having a fling with someone handsome/beautiful could be titillating and exhilarating. If you avoid the long-term costs of jeopardizing your valued marriage for the short-term advantage of temporary excitement, is this going to be satisfying to you?

Most avoidance is affect based. We do not want to feel a feeling (frequently anxiety, challenge and fear of failure, disapproval from important others, or anger).

Let's look at these polemics between short-term and long-term goals.

Short-Term Goal	Long-Term Goal
To feel safe	To feel freedom
To feel happy	To avoid situations that may cause sadness
To avoid conflict	To be loved
To be esteemed by others	Not to feel rejection by asking for more than you may get
To go to church each Sunday	To have a sense of community with others

| To feel joy in my life. | To avoid conflict, stress, and not feel sad |
| To avoid anxiety | To feel happy rather than sad, and not feel stress |

First, look from the right column, and read down. Are any of these goals "bad?" No. Most people want to feel safe, happy, avoid conflict, have some higher sense of purpose, experience joy in life and avoid anxiety. Now, look only at the left column. Are any of these goals "bad?" No. Again, we want to feel happy rather than sad, to feel included rather than excluded, to be a part of rather than apart from, to feel relaxation rather than stress. So, why are they at times in conflict (a choice, polemic, many times an either or choice)? Because sometimes you can't have them both simultaneously in the situations you confront (as in the first example: safety vs. freedom).

If you have social anxiety, it is most safe to stay at home and watch Netflix rather than go to an event that is available to you. But are you happy with watching Netflix and living your social life vicariously through a movie? It certainly works in the short term. But what about the long term? What about your self-esteem? What about what you want from life, or wish you had in your life?

We now examine how avoidance can be harmful to you. Perhaps you are a business executive. You have two doors to your office. One leads to a group of angry customers demanding answers to their irritations (my product does not work, it came damaged, it was overpriced and did not represent what they thought they were buying). The other door leads to your staff, who have been vigorously pressing you for increased wages, better working conditions, and promotions. You decide not to make a decision. Not to exit through either door. To sit there until both the customers and staff leave. Did you solve any problems? Certainly both the customers and staff (even more irritated because they were ignored the day before) will be back. Maybe you delayed the inevitable. But at what price, to both you and the company?

If you are depressed, staying in bed most of the day does not solve the problem. If you have a gambling problem, taking out a loan to pay your bad debts does not solve the problem. If your friend frequently irritates you but you mostly ignore it, how probable are you to stay with your friend over time? If you put off a school assignment because it is overwhelming, why would you believe it would be easier on another day?

What To Do: Identify situations where your avoidance interferes with your life.

Why To Do It: Accomplish your goals. Feel the way you want to without totally sacrificing your long-term happiness. Expose yourself to distress for a greater good.

How To Do It: Take a few deep breaths. Ask yourself about the biggest feelings you often want to avoid. Try to avoid your avoidance tendencies.

Example:

What I Avoid	Why I Avoid It	Consequence
Telling my husband I love him.	Then he wants sex.	He feels I don't love him.

What I Avoid	Why I Avoid It	Consequence

You have identified what you avoid and why. Now identify how to minimize the consequences (the "why" of the avoidance) and better accomplish your long-term goals.

Example continued:

Why I Avoid It	Decrease Negative And Increase Positive
He will want sex.	Honey. I love you very much. I just want to go to bed. We can have sex another day. I know this frustrates you. I wish we could always be in sync, but that is unrealistic.

Now it is your turn.

Why I Avoid It	Decrease Negative And Increase Positive

CHANGING YOUR PERSPECTIVE

Think of yourself as a photographer. If you take a photograph "head on" to the subject, it looks one way. If you take a photograph of the same subject slightly to the right, left, higher, lower, with better or different lighting you see the same subject differently. Life is obviously not a photograph. Life is ever changing, moving, fluid, dynamic, and vivid. Life offers a view that a photograph can only capture in one small frame.

Avoidance sometimes is powered by your fear of the situation itself. Or your interpretation of the consequences (which may not be correct), or probably most frequently not by your thoughts but by your assessment (or fear) of what it would ultimately mean to you. Excellent books have been written on how to change thoughts (Burns, 1980; McKay et al., 2011). So let's focus on feelings, usually fear.

Suppose you (Jimmy) are in high school and want to go to the prom. You don't want to miss out on what seems at the time a monumental milestone in your life. But shucks, you know you are gay. And you live in a geography where being gay is rarely accepted, and certainly not in your high school. Secretly you know this other guy (Adam) is also probably gay. (Maybe not, maybe he is just very shy and is afraid to ask any girl out. It does not matter to you; either way you are in the same boat.) It does not matter to you at the time because you want the happiness of going to the prom and you are not emotionally ready to come "out" for whatever reason. You have made a temporary compromise and decide to suggest to your friend, "How about I ask Jane and you ask Veronica to the prom?" He says no: "the prom is stupid."

You know in high school few if any feel that the prom is stupid ("stupid" is an adolescent way of saying 'I don't think I can do this'). So strategically you say, "Listen…I'll ask Veronica if she will go to the prom with you, and tell her if she says yes the four of us (Jane, Veronica, Adam and Jimmy) can all go together." There is safety in numbers.

This is changing perspective. Looking at a potentially impossible situation and seeing it differently.

Let's take another situation. You are 30 years old. You tell yourself "..old enough to know better." But you are pregnant. You don't believe in abortion, but you also feel the man who impregnated you would not be a good father. And you don't want to be a single mother. In fact, most of your life you devoted yourself to your career, and you liked it. It brought satisfaction, a sense of meaning, a sense of community with your coworkers, a sense of empowerment both as a woman but also just as a human being. You pride yourself (because others have told you so) that you make good decisions.

One of the many conflicts you experience is that you don't want to confide in your friends. "It would shatter both how they see me, and how I want to see myself," you tell yourself. So you keep quiet. But you know you can't put off a decision about what you will do. Soon it will be obvious, physically. What do you do?

Do you ruminate? Do you violate one of your rules (have others see you as strong, preserve your sense of dignity at all costs, sacrifice your career in service of motherhood, get an abortion and try to forget about it, etc.)?

You don't want some frequent but insensitive remarks to be made: "Why didn't you use a condom?" You don't want your values to be challenged (about abortion). You don't want to sacrifice your career (you know in your job it is next to impossible to climb up the corporate ladder and raise a child as a single mother), and you definitely know the father of the child is ill equipped to be in a sustained relationship.) What do you do?

Changing perspective is not always about making compromises, as in the first example. Sometimes it is about untangling very complicated values and the situations in which they are embedded.

Can this woman change her environment? Yes she can. She can change jobs. She can move away to another place. She can get different friends (so as not to hear their disapproval). Can she change her values? Yes, she can. She could see abortion as acceptable. She can see motherhood as a virtue. She can redefine what success itself means.

Whatever she eventually decides (to make compromise, to change her environment, to change her values, etc.) is almost beside the point. To change perspective means to look at things differently, by all angles. It does not predict any certain outcome. By exploration of self and values we have more (rather than less) with which to deal. It gives us a fuller picture. Whatever decision we decide to make will be more satisfying. We have lived life more fully.

What to Do: Identify situations where you think changing your perspective might be useful.

Why To Do It: Reappraisal may profitably increase your coping skills.

How To Do It: Pick a repetitive situation that annoys you, creates frustration, or is simply unsatisfying. Look at it differently in the second column and see if you are satisfied.

Example:

Painful/Annoying Situation	Reframe/Alternative Perspective
I call Tom at least twice a week. I let him talk for an hour or so. He never asks me how I'm doing, how I feel, or anything at all about me. Makes me angry and frustrated. I'll just stop calling him.	Tom is needy. I have reinforced his selfishness week after week, so he sees this as the norm; I've made it acceptable. I need to start the conversation by telling him how I feel.

Painful/Annoying Situation	Reframe/Alternative Perspective

_____	_____
_____	_____
_____	_____
_____	_____

Procrastination

Procrastination can be a large factor in increasing and sustaining unwanted feelings. By it you are putting things off because they are aversive or overwhelming. Similar to avoidance (when you avoid an anticipated negative event), with procrastination you periodically think about having to do something that needs doing (see this thought itself as an aversive event), but delay it. During the delay process you think about it perhaps many times. Each time you think about it, but delay, you experience a bit of stress. Examples include:

- Charging your phone (or taking your charger to work)
- Paying your bills when you have the money to pay them
- Calling the appliance repair company
- Scheduling your colonoscopy
- Revising your resume
- Checking the status of your retirement portfolio
- Studying for the final exam
- Returning an email response to an important client
- Making your husband's favorite dish that he requested months ago

There are a variety of reasons we procrastinate. Dealing only with immediate short-term goals and demands (what I refer to as "swatting flies") and sacrificing broad attention (either focusing just on the environment or just on our self) can prompt procrastination. Thinking mostly about the obstacles to accomplishing a task and not the avenues that could achieve them (lack of strategic thinking) can prompt procrastination. Or giving in to your feelings and not having your reason be an equally powerful source can be the cause. Whatever the cause, procrastination is a negative influence in our lives and inhibits skillfully using emotion regulation techniques.

Make a list of things you procrastinate about and identify the negative consequences.

What To Do: Attempt to identify areas that are compelling (frequent, long-standing, or have the most bothersome outcomes for you).

Why To Do It: It can provide perspective, later resulting in greater problem-solving skill.

How To Do It: Think about undone chores, areas where bad things happened and in retrospect you know could have been prevented.

Example:

Procrastinating Behavior	Negative Consequence
I didn't go to the gas station. I'm running around ragged trying to get as much done as possible.	Ran out of gas on the freeway. Waited 20 minutes for AAA. Was very late for a meeting I spent hours preparing for.

Procrastinating Behavior	Negative Consequence

Make a strategy to avoid the effects of procrastination in your life.

Example:

Procrastinating Topic From Previous Exercise	Strategy to Overcome
Put gas in the car.	Every Saturday morning I will fill up the car tank (make it a new habit for me) even though I may have half a tank in it already.

Procrastinating Topic From Previous Exercise	Strategy to Overcome

Rumination

Rumination is very different from procrastination. Rumination is when you have repetitive thoughts that get you nowhere. It is a circular thinking process, where you have a number of thoughts that are connected, perhaps even goal-directed, but the very fact that you repeat them over and over in your head is hurtful. It is hurtful because it clogs up your thinking process without a strategy to release or resolve the thoughts, interferes with your ability to focus on feelings that may be prompting the ruminative thoughts, and limits experience of the here and now. You are in your head too much, rather than being in the world. There is no strategy, just sentences in your head that are not predictive, heuristic, or useful.

When someone asks you a complex or difficult question you probably don't reply, "Let me ruminate on that a while." Instead you are more likely to say something like, "Let me sleep on that," or "Let me think that through."

Rumination is a rut. So what could be the underlying reason it happens at all? One simple explanation is the kindling effect (Gaito, 1974): once a set of brain neurons fire repeatedly, the probability of it re-firing increases. So it could be biological. Psychologically, the fear of making a mistake is so great that we take an issue and "work it to death" in the hope we will avert the perceived catastrophic possibilities. Whatever the cause, rumination makes unwanted feelings linger. And it may be related to the "development, maintenance, and recurrence of depression" (Sheppes, 2014).

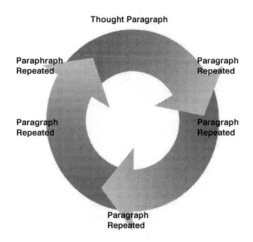

Figure 6: Ruminative Thinking Process

As the Figure 6 shows, rumination has no action phase, no termination or conclusion, and probably the only feeling is related to the distress of the rumination itself rather than any external event (even though the "thought paragraph" may be *about* some external event).

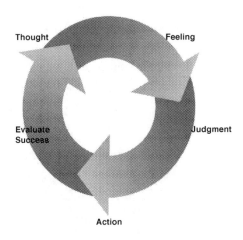

Figure 7: Nonruminative Thinking and Action Process

Figure 7 shows that without rumination we have a thought, it may bring a feeling that we mindfully (with curiosity and exploration) experience, then we decide if we want this thought and feeling to continue or not, which may lead to an action (to change the event prompting the cycle), and you finally evaluate how successful you were with that experience.

Here are some techniques to stop rumination:

Strategy	Examples
Response Interruption	Do something else (call someone and talk about *anything <u>but</u>* what you are ruminating about; take a cool shower; turn on a news program and recite the topic just covered to yourself; write a letter to a friend about anything except your rumination
Mindfulness	Focus on your senses and not your thoughts, especially strong senses
Distraction	Prepare a meal; sing a song; play a game of cards; go to a friend's house
Practice Self-Compassion	Say to yourself generous self-statements: "I share what I have." "I feel my bond with others." "I feel a part of my community." "I am thankful what I have" (and list all the things you are thankful for).
Expand Positive Experiences	Do work on your "Expand Positive Experiences Worksheet" on page 217

If you have problems with rumination, pick one of the strategies above (or any others that work for you), and develop a plan *prior* to being stuck in rumination. Anticipatory planning is helpful.

My Strategy for Rumination	What I Will Do
Distraction	I'm trying to learn to play the piano. I'm getting better with it after my lessons. I like it. Makes me feel good. I'll play the piano when I begin to ruminate.

My Strategy for Rumination	What I Will Do

Decentering

Decentering is "the act of disengaging from sensory, cognitive, or emotional phenomenon to achieve a psychological or reflective distance in relation to internal experiences" (Fresco, Segal & Buis, 2007). So decentering is about detaching from perceptions. Decentering is about detaching from your senses. Decentering is about detaching from your emotions. Decentering is a reflective process rather than a deepening one.

You might say to yourself, "Whoa, this is the opposite of the entire chapter on mindfulness that invited a welcoming attitude toward my experience." And you would be correct. But like mindfulness, decentering is designed to showcase the notion that feelings are transitory, temporary, ever changing, and momentary. Feelings come and go. Feelings are not facts (Farb et al., 2014). Unlike mindfulness, decentering diminishes rather than highlights experience.

The goal of decentering is to distance from your experience, and reappraise based on new postures in the situation you confront.

One way of decentering is to *watch yourself watching*. Examples would be, in your mind (not out loud), saying (and imagining as if you were an observer rather than the observed):

- "I see myself looking at my mother, listening to her criticizing me, and I am standing there looking and listening."
- "I see myself crying because my boyfriend did not call me. My hands are in my lap and tears are falling down my face. I look sad."
- "I see myself feeling pity for myself. I'm both ruminating and thinking a lot. The more I think the less pity for myself I feel."

So above you try to see your situation as if it is a movie or photograph. You engage in this process in order to psychologically distance yourself (decrease emotionality), and decrease the tendency for automatic reactiveness (that may make the situation worse).

Principles of Decentering

- Describe the situation as if you were watching yourself in the situation from a window looking in to the event.
- Articulate the situation as if you were telling someone else's story.

- Describe feelings, don't re-experience them or practice them. Just describe.
- Don't predict the future. Describe as if you were watching a movie, and not telling the ending before it happened.
- Describe details, but don't engage in a mini-novel: you are not entertaining, embellishing, or making the situation any more powerful than it is. Instead, like a good reporter, you report "this, then that, then the other thing."
- You don't state conclusions or interpretations. While you are engaging reason, you are not being so analytical that you "beat the horse to death" with analysis.
- It is simple explanation, from afar, and is not lengthy.

In the following exercise you are *practicing* how to decenter. You are not actually decentering because that occurs in the moment of experience. By practicing you will be better prepared to use this strategy in the moment.

What To Do: Identify highly emotional situations you want to change. Decenter from them.

Why To Do It: Shifts you from emotions in to thinking, from reactiveness in to reflectiveness, increasing problem solving and reduces emotional intensity.

How To Do It: While an emotionally provocative situation is occurring engage in the principles above.

Practice decentering using the principles listed above, so you are ready to use them when the situation occurs. Example:

Situation	Decentering
I'm being humiliated by three classmates who are telling me I am less than them.	I see the three classmates, their faces and their smug smiles saying mean things. Then I see those three people getting smaller and smaller, while I stay my same size. They get so small that they are now in the distance, barely perceptible. I can no longer hear or see them.
Somebody calls me a "nigger" and that I should know my "place" by now.	I look at his white face, his blue shirt, his ivory hat, and imagine him in white KKK robes. I see him burning innocent people's homes (the fire is red and fluid), and hanging black men from green-leafed trees because they had the audacity to speak as an equal. My image turns from color to black and white. Then it gets blurry. Then it becomes unintelligible. Then I hear the bigot's screams that he is being erased from my memory.
I'm making a PowerPoint presentation to business colleagues. At the end one of them (in public and in front of everyone) says, "You obviously have not researched this topic. You got it all wrong."	I imagine the offending colleague himself giving a presentation. First his projector won't work. Then he can't find his PowerPoint presentation. Then he fumbles his words. They all laugh at him, but I tell him "Well, we are not all prepared all the time, are we?" He looks angry while I feel satisfied.

Situation	Decentering

If you say to yourself that this process is not fair (the bullied classmate should punch them, the black man should spit on the white guy, and the PowerPoint lady should demean the man in the audience), I would have a variety of responses to those thoughts: life is frequently not fair, hatred does not breed love, "coming back at them with the same" usually escalates situations, and typically it is not strategic or focused on long-term goals.

This is one of the strategies that you need to do concurrent to the experience (like mindfulness). You can do it after the fact if you are stuck on an experience, but it is more helpful to do it in the here and now. The purpose is not to strike back, but to get distance and to soothe yourself.

Removing Yourself From The Situation

At times, feelings (either yours or others) can become so intense that effective coping strategies (even when you have many of them) simply don't work. High arousal (very strong feelings) can make us say or do things we later regret. You might make decisions that later, upon reflection, you regret. Interestingly, I've found that when others are very hostile or passionate and I say, calmly, "How curious that you are so worked up over this little matter," it makes matters worse. It is illogical but true that when someone else is very upset and you remain very calm and detached, they become enraged. It increases rather than decreases their volatility. (The same is not true for mild, modest, or only slightly elevated emotions: calm engenders calm.)

What to do? When situations become heated, it is probably good to take a "time out." I used it very successfully with my boys, when things were getting out of hand I would shout "Time Out!" and they knew discussion ended, action stopped, and they were to sit. They were not leaving the room or house (I'm not going to throw my little kids out of the house). In kind, when their discussion with me began to increase their emotions, I allowed them to leave the room (they were cooling off, and would come back later to negotiate). It works well with children and adolescents, why not with adults? Especially you.

It does not matter who is right or wrong, who is getting upset and who is not. When the situation spells high emotionality, you take the initiative to excuse yourself from the room. Say briefly "I need a break" and leave the room. Not surprisingly, such emotion-filled situations occur more frequently in families and other close-nit environments (roommates, boyfriend-girlfriend, and even in church elder settings). People are invested in these settings. They care. If a stranger is rude to you, you probably just walk away. You don't care about her or him. Families and other intimate environments are totally different.

Why should you take the responsibility to take the time out, to remove yourself from the environment, when you believe you were not the instigator or cause? We only have control over our own behavior, and only modest ability to influence the behavior of others. Also because I believe if you are doing these exercises and purchased this workbook you are motivated for change, and will eventually have superior coping skills compared to others.

Here are some things you might say prior to leaving the situation:

- This is getting out of hand.
- We can discuss this later when everyone is cooled off.
- I need a break from this.
- I understand we are upset, let's delay this for another time.
- This is important. I'll be back.

Notice the texture or attitude of these statements? They are not blaming. They use "I" statements rather than "You" statements. It does not diminish the importance of what is being discussed. It provides you a graceful exit.

How long should your break, leaving the situation, be? Depending on you, the person or people with whom you are dealing, it could be minutes (get a glass of water, tidy the kitchen, or make the bed) hours (go on an errand, make some phone calls, or pet your dog and groom her) or an entire day (have a "sleep over" with a friend). Measure it by the intensity of emotion. If you are talking about politics or religion, probably a shorter break is in order. If it is about personal historical events (who is at fault for this or that), then probably a medium break. If it goes to the core of the relationship or is extremely heated (name calling, threats, accusations), then maybe an over-night respite is required.

A good rule of thumb is to take your time out early in the process. Rather than saying "Not that again," say "Whoa, we need to work on this for a long time. It is not going to happen overnight." Removing yourself from the situation early, even briefly, will help the situation from escalating beyond control.

Here are the functions of removing yourself from the situation:

- It is a response interrupter: the chain of events is broken, even if temporarily.
- It can reduce emotional intensity, if done properly.
- It gives you time to think about what has been said, without having to defend yourself.
- You can think of new strategies that may be more effective.
- Is a concrete demonstration that interpersonal problems are *processes (that may take time to resolve)*. It is unlike a legal contract that is either signed, negotiated, or refused.

Think of the triggers that are most frequent in situations you confront that may prompt you to leave the situation.

What To Do: Identify triggers and situations associated with them.

Why To Do It: Prepares you to see patterns, cope better, and use the technique to effectively remove yourself from the situation.

What To Do: Think of the three most volatile times emotions have erupted, and give them a brief label. State the situation that caused the trouble (the context and issues involved).

Example:

Triggering Topic	Context and Issues Involved

Money	My husband spends too much money. He wants all these tools, which he says he needs. When I say no, the baby needs milk and we need to start a savings account, he flips out.
Sex	My wife does not want sex frequently enough. They say men just want sex and don't engage in romance, but I romance her, tell her how much I love her, help around the house, and she is just never in the mood for lovemaking.
Childrearing	Our kids are out of control. They don't want to do their small chores, they think the world should always revolve around them, and one of us needs to be the disciplinarian. Neither of us wants to be the "bad guy." We both want to be the loving parent. And look what it's doing to our kids!

Triggering Topic	Context and Issues Involved

As in the examples, these are volatile situations: money, sex, and childrearing standards are among the most contentious situations in a relationship (plus jealousy). They do not resolve themselves overnight or in one discussion. But tempers flare. Identify how you plan to gracefully remove yourself from the situations you listed.

What To Do: Identify exit plans from extreme conflict.

Why To Do It: Having a plan *prior* to conflict is thoughtful, strategic, and increases your probabilities of success.

How To Do It: Use the same trigger topics as before in the first column. Articulate a reasonable plan to take a time out, have a strategy, and reassure the people with whom you are dealing that you are taking the situation seriously.

Triggering Topic	Plan For Removing Myself
Money	We are both hot under the collar over this. Let's take a hiatus for one week from this situation. I need to go help Uncle Henry with his washing machine. I'll be back in a few hours. Next week we will develop a budget, with all our expenses and income. And not talk about specific purchases until we've done the budget.
Sex	This is an emotionally charged issue. I'm moving in with my brother for a week. I'll come by after work and we can visit for an hour. I'm not leaving you. I just think we need a break. If that doesn't work, let's go to counseling.
Childrearing	I'm angry about this. Every time we talk about the kids we get extremely upset. I'm afraid this is going to lead to divorce if we don't come to a resolution. I'm going shopping for a few hours. When I return let's work with pencil and paper on principles we agree on, and deal with the specific behaviors the kids display later.

Triggering Topic	Plan For Removing Myself

Remove Yourself From Dangerous Situations

Some things we should not tolerate, and denial, avoidance, decentering, taking a break, and changing perspective are unacceptable. In denial you essentially say to yourself "This is not happening." In changing perspective we are giving the situation "the benefit of the doubt." The difference between avoidance and removing yourself from the situation is that avoidance is about not wanting to confront feelings maybe you should, but there are situations that are absolutely unacceptable by any circumstances. How do you tell the difference? Unacceptable situations include:

- When you are in physical danger (hitting, kicking, choking, etc.)
- When someone you care about is in physical danger
- When you clearly know another's behavior towards you is malicious and evil

- When someone threatens you with physical harm
- When someone attempts or does rape or sexually molests you
- When someone attempts to blackmail you
- When your own anger reaches the level that you have a malicious or evil intent towards another
- When you see a potentially lethal situation in your immediate area

This is the one and only exercise that I hope will be left blank because you are not in a dangerous situation. If you are, check which of the following you plan to do to remove yourself from danger:

	Call 911
	Ask for a police escort to leave the premises
	Call local battered women's shelter or call your local crisis center
	Call an ambulance
	Make arrangements to stay with a friend or relative until you have a long-term plan

Focus on the Body

Distress resides both in the mind and in the body. When we become distressed our breathing becomes short and shallow, we may have temperature changes (body feeling cold because the blood is constricted from your arms, hands, feet; or hot because our heart rate increases flowing warmth throughout your body). You've heard the expression "she looks pale" or "he looks flushed."

Our muscles tend to tighten, as if prepared for battle or to run away from danger. Frequently, once the muscle tighten they don't "let go" even when you feel calmer than before. Techniques of muscle relaxation and breathing relaxation have good experimental evidence to support them (Berking & Schwartz, 2014).

Deep Breathing

Since the body changes how we breathe under stress (becoming short and shallow, rapid rather than regular, erratic rather than rhythmic), one way to stop unwanted feelings is to intervene directly in your body. The reason our breathing changes under stress has to do with the fight or flight dynamic. Remember that our bodies were designed to avoid threatening situations. Historically a threat was some kind of beast or another person who presented immediate physical danger. Breathing changes so that increased oxygen is pumped through the blood to prepare for battle or to run to safety. Nowadays most threats are ambiguous, socially determined, and fluid. Rather than a beast or predator, we confront cognitive and social threats. You can't pay the bills, you didn't get the promotion, your father is driving you nuts, you may fail chemistry and you hoped to become a doctor, your husband won't answer the phone when he is at work, or you just can't finish the vision for the piece of art you had in mind.

Our bodies, however, react to these cognitive and social threats as if they were the predator beast; as if it is an immediate threat and immediate action can solve it.

Here are the *Steps in Deep Breathing:*

1. Notice the impaired breathing before attempting to change it. Is it short and shallow, or rapid and you feel like you can't catch your breath?
2. Take one deep breath. Pause for one second before you exhale.
3. Take a second deep breath. Feel the temperature of the air entering your nostrils. Pause one second before exhale. Notice the temperature of the air leaving your nostrils.
4. Continue with steps two and three. Notice over time the rhythm of your breathing. Does it feel too slow or too fast? Focus on the sensation itself of breathing.

5. Mindfully pay attention to other areas of your body associated with your breathing: the rising and falling of your chest as your lungs inflate and deflate, the air that enters your belly, if you feel temperature or other changes in your face, hands, and feet.

6. Again focus on rhythm. See breathing as a circular process that is even, steady, repetitive, and comforting.

7. After three minutes of this focused attention on your breathing (steps 2 – 6), split your attention between the breath and imagine the oxygen entering your red blood cells and replenishing every area of your body. Nourishment for your body; nourishment for your soul. Do this for one minute.

8. Finally, as you focus on your breath and its rhythm, say to yourself upon each inhale one or more of the following words: calm, relaxed, soothed, comfort, safe, secure, protected, loving, care-filled, eased.

Practice deep breathing now.

What to Do: Deep Breathing

Why to Do It: Relax, have a strategy to decrease body reactions to stress. Change an unwanted feeling in to a wanted one.

How To Do It: Read the eight steps above three times (so you don't have to look at the steps while you are deep breathing). Engage in the steps. Don't worry if you are following exactly in the sequence of steps. They are guidelines. Write the date, place a check mark when completed, and journal how it felt. Do it at least once per day for the next 10 days.

Example:

Date	How I Felt
8/3	Felt more relaxed. Pleased.
8/4	Didn't work as well as yesterday, but I do feel more relaxed.
8/5	Didn't do it today. Disappointed.

Date	How I Felt

As the example above shows, you will not always get exactly the same result each time you do the exercise. The reason is that what went on before (how many different stressors, how intense or lengthy they were, etc.) as well as what is going on now (how distracted you are, how rushed you feel, what kind of expectations—appraisals—you have) will effect outcome. Nevertheless, deep breathing is a well-established and centuries old procedure from which most benefit. Use it regularly despite momentary failures. It is meant to be preventive and protective, and it will work if you use it regularly.

Muscle Relaxation

When your muscles tighten you are prepared to fight or flee. This is not relaxation; it feels bad. There are two major strategies for reducing muscular tension to be reviewed. The first is progressive muscle relaxation and the second is the body scan method. You need not do both, pick one. Use the Progressive Method if you know you carry stress in your muscles. If you don't think you do carry tension in your muscles, still do the Body Scan periodically. They are different but both attempt to achieve muscle relaxation. Even if you do not feel a sore back, jaw, or neck (or any other body part) as a result of extreme muscle tension, these procedures can help you relax.

Moreover, body tension is typically a slow and escaling process. You tend not to recognize it until you feel muscle pain. Better to prevent it than allow that to happen to you.

Steps and Guidelines for Progressive Muscle Relaxation:

1. Relax in a chair or on the floor.
2. Tighten each muscle group as hard as you can, almost painfully, for 10 seconds. All of a sudden, immediately, relax that muscle group.
3. Notice the tension in the muscles, mindfully, for those ten seconds.

4. When that particular muscle group is relaxed after the 10 seconds, wait 15 seconds and mindfully notice how the muscle feels in relaxation after exertion.

5. If during the relaxation period you continue to feel tension, repeat for that same muscle group steps 2 – 4.

6. Go through each muscle group in the chart below, one group at a time. For each muscle group it is 10 seconds of tightening, and 10 seconds of mindfully noticing the difference between tightening and relaxation. Repeat steps 2 – 5 for each muscle group.

7. Finally, after the exercise is over, notice any remaining tension in a particular muscle group and give that muscle group special attention on another day when you again do this exercise.

Muscle Group	What To Do
Hands	Clench them in to a fist. First the right for 10 seconds, then the left for ten seconds.
Wrists and forearms	Extend them, and bend your hands back at the wrist. Stretch the muscles as hard as you can for 10 seconds.
Biceps and upper arms	Clench your hands into fists, bend your arms at the elbows towards yourself, and flex your biceps.
Shoulders	Shrug them (raise toward your ears). Hold it tightly for ten seconds.
Forehead	Wrinkle it into a deep frown. Make the muscles as tight as you can.
Around the eyes and bridge of the nose	Close your eyes as tightly as you can. (Remove contact lenses before you start the exercise.)

Cheeks and jaws	Smile as widely as you can. Make it exaggerated.
Around the mouth	Press your lips together tightly. (Check your face for tension. You just want to use your lips.)
Back of the neck	Press your head forwards towards your chest for 10 seconds, tightly. Then rest. Then press your neck and head tightly toward your right shoulder for 10 seconds, then rest. Press your neck and head tightly toward your left shoulder, then rest.
Front of the neck	Touch your chin to your chest. (Try not to create tension in your neck and head.)
Chest	Take a deep breath, and hold it for 4 to 10 seconds. Push your chest out in an exaggerated way. Then relax.
Back	Arch your back up and away from the floor or chair.
Stomach	Suck it into a tight knot. (Check your chest and stomach for tension.)
Hips and buttocks	Press your buttocks together tightly. Hold it for 10 seconds.
Thighs	Clench them hard.
Legs	Stretch your legs as much as you can outward from your body for 10 seconds, then relax.

Lower legs	Point your toes toward your face for 10 seconds. Rest. Then point your toes away, and curl them downward at the same time for 10 seconds. (Check the area from your waist down for tension.)

Adapted from Healthwise, University of Michigan Health System, 2018.

What To Do: Go through all of the muscle groups in the chart above.

Why To Do It: Increases relaxation, highlights the role and consequence of muscle tension in distress.

How To Do It: Carefully and mindfully follow the instructions for each muscle group, following the steps and guidelines above. Do it once or twice per week. Record your progress below.

Example:

Date	What I Felt and Thought
8/3	It hurts tensing these muscles. It takes a lot of time.
8/10	Hurts muscles, but not as much as last time. Still takes a chuck out of my day.

| 8/16 | I really notice now when my muscles begin to tense (not just when I'm doing my exercise). Makes me aware of how my stress is affecting my body. |

Date	What I Felt and Thought

Body Scan

Body scan is very similar to progressive muscle relaxation but does not involve tightening and relaxing of the muscles. In the Body Scan you simply mindfully notice how your muscles are feeling (relaxed or tense) in each area for a few seconds, then go on to the next group of muscles and do the same. Like with the Progressive Muscle Relaxation exercise it is designed to sensitize you to your muscles, identify tension where it exists, and to simply encourage your muscles to relax.

Guidelines for Body Scan:

1. Relax in a chair or on the floor.
2. Notice each muscle group as mindfully as you can before going to the next muscle group.
3. Notice any tension in the muscles, and focus on them until they feel more relaxed.
4. Mindfully notice how the difference between muscle tension and muscle relaxation.
5. Finally, after the exercise is over, notice any remaining tension in a particular muscle group and give that muscle group special attention on another day when you again do this exercise.

Do it for each of the muscle groups:

Muscle Group
Hands
Wrists and forearms
Biceps and upper arms
Shoulders
Forehead
Around the eyes and bridge of the nose
Cheeks and jaws
Around the mouth
Back of the neck
Front of the neck
Chest

Back
Stomach
Hips and buttocks
Thighs
Lower legs

Acceptance and Tolerance

Acceptance is one of the easiest to describe, and one of the most difficult to do. This is so because the situation is unchangeable, and should not be changed. Examples include loss through death of a loved one, loss through death of a pet, getting older, having a genetically-caused heart condition, accepting defeat in a task that allows no re-match, or being born in Ethiopia rather than Europe. You should not struggle to change the situation because you can't. You should not change your feelings about the situation because they are valid and reasonable reactions to unwanted events.

How do you practice acceptance when you are hurting? I wish I could present some heretofore unknown insight. I can't. Acceptance is about "biting the bullet," resigning yourself to the feelings you have and not struggling with them. Saying things to yourself like "This is wrong and I don't deserve it," only serves to make you feel worse. If you do that you are engaging in secondary feelings (Marra, 2004, 2005). Then you have two feelings with which you need to deal (the original feeling and the feeling about the feeling you have).

Acceptance is difficult. Rather than seeing it as "resigning" to bad feelings, frame it as accepting the inevitable. You are not wrong to feel bad about bad events that happen. In fact, it is correct to feel badly about bad events. It is human. It is natural.

Tolerance follows acceptance. Once a feeling is accepted, then you must engage in tolerating the unwanted feelings without unconsciously and unintentionally increasing them. How do you tolerate? You don't use many of the strategies in this workbook, you use a new one: "I have this feeling. Feelings come and go." This one is long-lasting for a reason (what brings the feeling was an event or situation that had great meaning). The meaning was not transitory or fleeting, so this feeling is not going to be short-lived or insignificant. We have to validate or allow the burden as lifelike processes we all face. It is not easy; it hurts. Struggling with it, rather than accepting and tolerating it, will make it hurt worse.

Practice acceptance and tolerance.

What To Do: Identify feelings that can't or should not be changed. Describe how you will practice acceptance and tolerance.

Why To Do It: It prevents inevitable bad feelings from becoming worse.

How To Do It: Select a feeling that is unwanted, but a reasonable reaction to an undesired event. The event should not be subject to alteration by means other than divine intervention (that you don't expect anyway.)

Example:

Situation	Acceptance and Tolerance
After 20 years of marriage my wife died of cancer, she was only 50 years old.	I feel pain at her loss. I feel anger that she died so young. I feel lost that I have to live alone. I miss her. I will always miss her. I feel love for the great times we had together. I feel sadness about the difficult times we had together. I feel sadness for me. I feel sadness for her. I feel sadness. Sometimes I feel I should go too (maybe we could be together in some spiritual realm, but I know my wife would slap me in the face if she heard me say that). She would want to see me mourn her loss because she understands the great love we had for each other. My feelings represent the power and value of our love. I will kiss her in my thoughts every day. I will feel without destroying myself emotionally

Situation	Acceptance and Tolerance

In this chapter we have reviewed the following strategies to have unwanted feelings linger less:

- Avoid:
  - Denial
  - Avoidance
  - Procrastination
  - Rumination

- Engage in the following:
  - Balance short- and long-term goals
  - Changing Perspective
  - Decentering
  - Removing yourself from the situation
  - Body Techniques
    - Deep Breathing
    - Muscle Relaxation
    - Progressive Muscle Relaxation
    - Body Scan
  - Acceptance and Tolerance

THE NATURE OF MAPS

You know what a map is all about. But think about the various kinds of maps there are. There are topographical maps. Topographical maps show elevation, sometimes in great detail, expressed through contour lines, contour interludes, and follow a series of mapmaking rules:

> The rule of Vs: sharp-pointed vees shapes made by contour lines usually represent stream valleys, where the drainage channel passes through the point of the vee, with the vee pointing upstream. This is a consequence of erosion.

> The rule of Os: closed loops are frequently uphill on the inside and downhill on the outside, and the innermost loop is often highest area or the lowest area.

Density of contours: closely spaced contours indicate a steep slope; distant contours a shallow slope. Two or more contour lines merging suggests a cliff. By calculating the number of contours that cross a segment of a stream, the stream gradient can be approximated.

When you look at a contour map, you are looking straight down at a representation of the Earth, so it is difficult to identify changes in elevation. Contour maps use contour lines to indicate height and maybe, more importantly, changes in elevation across the terrain.

– Mapscaping, 2019

Here are examples:

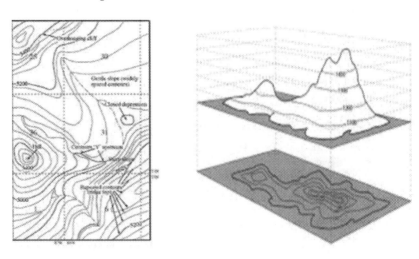

--Digitalatlas.cose.isu.edu   --Greenbelly.co

Figure 8: Contour Maps

Then there are roadmaps, which define freeways, highways, and streets. You are most familiar with these:

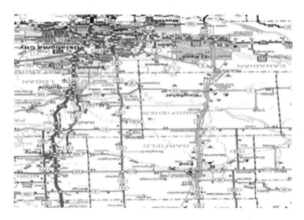

Figure 9: Street Maps Courtesy of State of Oklahoma

Then there are aerial maps:

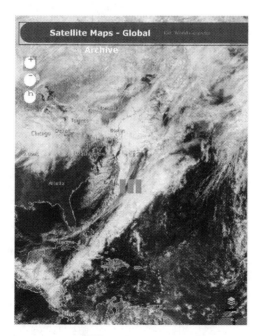

Figure 10: Aerial Map (NOAA) National Oceanic and Atmospheric Administration

There are also political maps, physical maps, climatic maps, and even customizable maps available on the internet.

Maybe you are asking what this has to do with feelings and how to change them, wisdom, or the aim of this book? The path of wisdom demands we know not only in what direction we are headed, but what the obstacles will be, where the simplest route will be, and even more importantly whether we really want to go to that destination at all.

There is an old saying in the field of linguistics: the map is not the territory (Hayakawa & Hayakawa, 1991). It has several meanings. At times we can get caught up in our words. When I say "love" it may mean something very different to you than it does to me. If you say "let's take separate cars" then you take a shortcut, and I'm slowed by traffic lights and traffic itself, and then I get lost, you may be furious at me. "I told you were to go, all you had to do was follow me." The map is not the territory also alludes to the critical function of language itself (interpretation, cultural factors, denotation versus connotation, and so forth).

I remember in graduate school I called something "precious." I thought it was innocuous. My fellow graduate students jumped verbally all over me like I had murdered someone. The word precious to them was a derogatory term meaning affectedly concerned with elegant behavior or manner. To me it meant valuable, treasured, and important. Words mean different things to different people. All you have to do is consult a dictionary and see the varied meanings the same word can have, even if the word is being used correctly to communicate what we are trying to say.

Any self-help book is particularly prone to misinterpretation. One reader of one of my former books accused me of being "anti-medication" because I did not address it as fully as behavioral issues. My defense is that I'm a psychologist, not a psychiatrist, do not have prescription privileges (as some psychologists do), and my book was about emotions and behavior, not the full encyclopedia of mental health care and research. Which introduces the entire notion of the complexity of being human.

If you try to help your daughter do her homework, you think you are being helpful. She may say and feel that instead you are being "restrictive," "belittling," "a nag," and just plain ole "mean."

We can get lost in words. If someone says to you "we have to have a 'come to Jesus' talk" that could mean anything. It can mean the person intends to verbally rip you to shreds, or maybe only that they want to discuss values. So if we prepare for attack (get defensive) even before the conversation begins you can imagine how the conversation will go (down hill). That is why conversations with our loved ones can be so lengthy, at times exhausting, and almost always time consuming but necessary. We may have to use four, five, six words to convey what we really intend. And we may have to use several examples, not just one, to get our point across.

THE NATURE OF WINING AND COMPETITION

When I was in high school I was on the debate team. The topic of the next year's debate was announced the year before. There was one topic all year. And we had to spend the summer researching *evidence* (not just opinions) for both sides of the argument (pro and con). We wrote debate cards that cited the evidence and the source. Then, within minutes of the debate, on the flip of a coin we were told what side we were on, pro or con. The pro side had 5 minutes to deliver their side. Followed by the con side which also had 5 minutes. Followed by 2 minutes of rebuttal for each side. The "judges" were typically attorneys and judges from the community who volunteered their time. It was exciting and fun. The debate team became a community, fulfilling both social and academic purposes. We learned critical thinking, maintaining poise even in the face of opposition, dispassionate discourse, and camaraderie. It was inherently rewarding. I received a full 4 year tuition scholarship to the University of the Pacific as a result.

College debate was different. The emphasis was on winning. We were coached on technique and strategy. There was less camaraderie, more pressure, less fun. I dropped out of debate (fortunately I had a college scholarship from the State as well, and was not economically handcuffed to the team).

Perhaps you have had similar experiences. You joined a civic or philanthropic organization and in the beginning it was fun, then it became work and effortful. Or you joined a church or synagogue, and in the beginning it was fulfilling and meaningful, until the demands for money and the politics of the congregation became overwhelming. Or your new relationship with your boyfriend was accepting and joyful, only to become over time too filled with demands for sex, and jealousy over your other friendships and activities.

To win is an objective. Competition means someone wins and someone loses. That is fine in many arenas in life, like sports. In personal endeavors, however, competition can be destructive. You can lose the sense of meaning and purpose you seek. That is particularly true in relationships. One-upmanship (where you always try to 'out do' the other person) can have negative consequences, and makes a relationship effortful.

There are lessons from debate applicable to good human discourse. You have to listen and understand the other side, which means among other things, that you don't interrupt. You hear them out. If you go on and on endlessly and repeat yourself, maybe saying something like "Let me know when you are finished and I'll respond," you are telling the person you want to win rather than understand. If you are going to disagree with someone, don't start with your conclusion ("You are wrong."). Instead perhaps say, "Interesting, I see it from another perspective." If the goal is to win, and you are in a relationship or family, someone is going to lose.

BACK TO THE MAPS: DENIAL

Winning and competition are not the right map for relationships. Let's say the topographical. In terms of goals, it tells you your obstacles. How hard you need to climb, or how you need to avoid. Perhaps the biggest hurdle of all is denial. In denial you refuse to believe there is a mountain to climb, or that maybe YOU are the mountain. Denial is very tricky, because by definition it is invisible and disbelieved. But it is all too common.

Examples:

"I don't have an anger issue! Why do keep saying that?"
"Why do you keep calling me on my stuff? What about your stuff?"
"What do you mean I have intimacy issues? I'm just sick of tired of that phrase."
"You whine too much about the same old things. Bring up something new!"
"You seem to be a broken record. You keep repeating yourself."

Or the political map:
"You keep trying to draw boundaries, as you call it. Let's just do it my way for once."
"It's my way or the highway."
"I'll see you in court."

Or the street map:
"Your way is just not working for me."
"You make things more difficult than they need to be."
"Just follow my directions. Stop arguing with me."
"Don't you have a moral compass? You want me to be somebody I'm not."

Or climatic maps:

"You're never in the mood!"

"I can't talk to you when you are this way."

"You're just too emotional."

"Why do you always cry when you don't get your way?"

The physical map is subtle, but powerful, like the rest:

"If you would lose a few pounds you'd be attractive."

"Your penis is too big."

"Have you considered breast enhancement?"

"I've seen ads for wrinkle removal. Have you considered that?"

All of these metaphorical maps bring to mind multiple issues: judgmentalism, acceptance, gender factors, relationship factors, cultural factors, individual differences, discrimination, critical thinking, strategic behavior, the nature of conflict, context, and a myriad of other issues.

You may be using the wrong intrapersonal (within yourself) or interpersonal (between you and others) map to make wise decisions.

What To Do: Identify situations where you were using the wrong filter or map to define a situation or problem.

Why To Do It: It can increase flexibility in your problem-solving process and help you see more than one way of looking at the same problem.

How To Do It: Think of a situation you were "barking up the wrong tree" or one where the eyeglasses or lens through which you were or are viewing a problem is incorrect.

From the examples above, list two ways you have found that the map or filter through which you were viewing a problem was the wrong one. Better yet, think of a problem in the here-and-now where you may be using the wrong map to solve a problem.

Example:

Situation	Old Map	New Map
Wife may be cheating on me.	Lens of jealousy. Map was that a woman's place was in the home, and she frequently was not home.	Lens of understanding. She told me her elderly parents needed a lot of assistance. With my complaints, she had me go over to their home with her and see how much time they really needed (cleaning their home, buying groceries, taking them to doctor appointments, etc.). They need her too.

Situation	Old Map	New Map

This chapter is about schemas, maps, belief systems, ways of thinking rooted in pre-conceived notions that may, or may not, be true. It is also about clarity of goals and purpose. Maybe my map, of my way getting from here to there, is flawed to begin with because I really didn't want to get from here to there in first place, and just blindly followed the map because it was the only map I had handy to me at the time.

Now, on to context and the role of decision making, context in defining the self, and then finally exploring the path of wisdom.

CONTEXT AND SELF

What is context? Context is about connection, to weave together, a connected structure, a coherence between parts, and the bearing of the parts to the whole (OED, 2001). And what is self? That is even more complicated; the OED devotes nine pages to it (pages 905- 913, Volume XIV, 2001)! Here is the short version: "self is the primary same, the sense of 'same,' the sense of identity that comes from the confluence of many factors, one's own, it is a conjunction, a combination, that which is intrinsically *he*; the ego "...often identified with the soul or mind as opposed to the body...a permanent subject of successive and varying states of consciousness" (page 907). So self is about identity, nature, character, dispositions, and interests.

If these two ideas, context and self, are woven together you see the complexity and richness that can be used to define one's path of wisdom. Since complexity is there, but difficult with which to deal in any holistic sense apart from philosophy (which this book is not about), we have to break it down into specific components. We break context down in to the most frequently viewed contextual formats: family, culture, neighborhood, and the jobs and roles we perform. We break self down into values, spirituality, desires, and predispositions. We have to compare and analyze the relationship of context and self. It is unlikely that one will pursue a course (even if that course is initially enticing) that is contrary to your culture, roles, values, and predispositions. They go together like the pieces of a puzzle.

FAMILY CONTEXT

Think of family in a broad context. Perhaps you moved away from your family of origin years ago. You may live in a different state, county, or even country than your family of origin, or even your immediate family. However, it is important nonetheless to assess each of these variables. (If for no other reason that our early childhood experiences last a long time.) Look at the list below, and rate how each variable is of importance to you. If the item is not applicable to you, leave it blank.

Rating Scale
- 5 = I absolutely dislike this role/factor
- 4 = I strongly dislike this role/factor
- 3 = I dislike this role/factor
- 2 = I sort of dislike this role/factor
- 1 = I almost dislike this role/factor
+ 1 = I almost like this role/factor
+ 2 = I sort of like this role/factor
+ 3 = I like this role/factor
+ 4 = I strongly like this role/factor
+ 5 = I absolutely like this role/factor

Family Role	Rating
Younger Brother/Sister #1	
Younger Brother/Sister #2	
Younger Brother/Sister #3	
Older Brother/Sister #1	
Older Brother/Sister #2	
Older Brother/Sister #3	
Father	
Mother	
Maternal Grandparent	
Paternal Grandparent	
Aunt	
Uncle	
Godmother/Godfather	
Other:	

NEIGHBORHOOD

Possible Value	Rating
Living in the area that is familiar to me (where I grew up, spent the longest time, or have the most friends or family)	
Living in a low crime area, even if it means moving.	
Living near nature (lake, ocean, trees, grass, hills, mountains, etc.)	
Convenience (shopping, school, church, job, etc.)	
Other:	

CULTURE

In a fascinating book chapter on culture (Mesquita, De Leersnyder & Albert, 2014) the authors describe how people have cultural models that shape their behavior and their problem solving style. In one culture tolerance, acceptance, and harmony is the model. In another culture the focus is on accomplishments. In another it is focused on shame for transgressions. Similarly, perceptions or appraisals differ with culture. The authors describe how a woman, getting attention from a man who is not her husband, react differently depending on culture: "[it will] differ depending on whether her culture construes such attention as an honor violation, a sign that she is attractive, or a marker that she is being objectified in a sexist world."

There are also "display rules" (Mesquita, De Leersnyder & Albert, 2014) for what kind of emotions are acceptable to exhibit. In many European and American cultures expressions of happiness are allowed, while East Asians tend to avoid such expressions. Suppression of emotions seems to be effortful in European Americans but not in Asian Americans or East Asians. Hong-Kong Chinese appear comfortable with suppression of emotions, but not Americans.

They (Mesquita, De Leersnyder & Albert, 2014) describe the work of one anthropologist who studied (historically) the Phillippe Ilongots and found that harmony (that excluded strong feelings) within the tribe was so intense that if disharmony was experienced tribal members would seek out non-tribe members to behead in order to discharge their own anger and energy. What these authors conclude is that one critical factor is that in some cultures independence is rewarded and in others interdependent values are rewarded.

Culture gets a little more complex because it involves dominant belief systems of your country, your nationality, your religious background, and other factors. Using the same rating scale as for family above, rate each of the dimensions below.

Possible Values of Country in Which I Live	Rating
My country, right or wrong!	
Commitment to my country means I respect and comply with rituals (such as allegiance to the flag, respecting national holidays, etc.)	
It is a must that I vote in order to have my voice heard.	
My elected or appointed leaders must be shown respect, even if I disagree with their viewpoints.	
To dissent, to have an opposing viewpoint, is my right.	
I must watch the national news or study other media in order to make an informed decision.	
Citizenship is less important than basic respect for others.	
Just as long as I am left alone, I don't care about politics.	
If I vote, I vote. I don't care about national matters all that much.	
Principles above politics.	
Other:	

Nationality Values	Rating
I may have been born here, but my "roots" are from elsewhere.	
My family strongly emphasized that the "old ways" are more important than what might be popular around me.	
It is important to protect the values of my nation.	
My nationality is unimportant to me.	
Other:	

Religious Values	Rating
My religious beliefs are very defining of how I see myself.	
I go to my church, synagogue, temple, sanctuary, or prayerful house of assembly fairly regularly.	
When I have to choose between my religious beliefs and what is more expedient, I try to always follow my religious doctrine.	
I find sustenance in being surrounded by people with similar religious beliefs.	
Hearing a good sermon is very inspiring to me.	
I pray regularly.	
I try to gently sway others to develop their spiritual potential.	
I judge others when they express sacrilegious beliefs or behavior.	
Prayer and religion is a waste of time.	
I am impressed when I meet someone who, although not forceful, lives the principles they say they believe in.	
Other:	

Other Cultural Expressions	Rating
When I see others dress in garb that is different from what I am accustomed to (Kippah, shalu sharma, Hijab, Niqab, ruband, turban, etc.) I feel uncomfortable.	
People should adopt the country's ways they live in.	
I absolutely avoid doing anything that might disgrace my family.	
I believe in tolerance for other cultural beliefs and customs.	

I believe in the "melting pot" theory: adapt to the majority.	
Other:	

Let's put together what we have so far. Find the +5 ratings (if you have many of them, just pick a few) from each of the categories above.

What To Do: Identify your strong likes, and your strong dislikes.

Why To Do It: It will help you live a values-based life.

How To Do It: In the next section, pick your +5 ratings, and in the following section identify your -5 ratings. Write why.

Example of my + 5:

Role/Values/Culture	Why It Is Important to Me
Grandmother	She is fun to be around, let's me know I did a good job with my children
Country: Principles above politics.	We just need to love one another. Live and let live.
Cultural: Tolerance	People are just people. They were raised different than I was. As long as they are good to me and mine. Live and let live.

Role/Values/ Culture	Why It Is Important to Me

Now deal with your -5:

Role/Values/Culture	Why It Is Unimportant to Me
Family: Uncle	He thinks he knows everything, and he tells me so every time I see him. It is annoying.
Country: Show respect to leaders even when they are wrong.	Corruption and egotistical thinking, hate-ism...we have to express our disgust directly to them so they don't think they can get away with it.
Cultural: Melting Pot	Yes, we are a diverse nation and I think everyone should know how to speak English, but I don't believe other cultures should abandon their historical identities and roots just to fit in.

Role/Values/Culture	Why It Is Unimportant to Me

JOB/EMPLOYMENT/CAREER

I change the rating scale for this one. Employment or money-making involves such a vast resource time for most of you. For some it may be part-time, but for most it is full-time. And for many when issues such as travel time, preparation, and the education necessary prior to obtaining employment, it involves more than an 8-hour per day investment. If you are unemployed or underemployed it may feel even worse to you.

Examine this rating scale carefully. Attempt to be honest with yourself, and take a long-term rather than short-term evaluation of this ranking system. (If you lost your job yesterday obviously you feel distraught. Think about before then, when you were working. If you are a student and have not yet begun your work, anticipate what it might feel like once you are employed). If you ask where the negative numbers are, the answer is probably you need to rethink your career plans.

Rating Scale:
0 = I disagree.

1 = I agree a little bit.

2 = I agree.

3 = I agree a lot.

4 = I agree whole heartedly.

Statement	Rating
My job is one of the most important defining criteria about who I think I am as a person.	
I would be lost without my job.	
I get satisfaction with the people with whom I interact on my job.	
The content (what I actually do) I enjoy.	
I look forward to going to work, even though I enjoy vacations and off- time as well.	
My work is meaningful to me.	
I get pride when discussing my work with others.	
I think others respect me for the work I do.	
Sometimes I feel my work is effortless.	
I would choose this line of work again, if I had it to do over again.	
I would recommend my line of work to others who have similar interests.	

ADD YOUR RANKINGS TOTAL:

If you are absolutely thrilled with your job, congratulations, you likely scored near 44. If you scored 40 you are still doing great. If you scored between 33 and 39, you are happy. If you scored around 20 or above, you are satisfied. If you scored below 11 you know you are dissatisfied. Work is important, but so are so many other areas of life.

THE OTHER ROLES YOU PERFORM

We all perform multiple roles or functions in life. Some of them are necessary but perhaps not that enjoyable (like taking out the trash), and some of them full of zest and excitement (like sex or a really great movie). Some of them are rather thoughtless (like putting on your shoes before going outside on a stormy night), while others are effortful (like studying for a test, preparing for a job interview, or trying to plan a surprise party for a loved one).

It is easy to get lost in one role (say, for example, being a student when having good grades seems like the one thing you *should* do, or preparing for a date when you want your first impression to be mind boggling, or preparing your final arguments as a criminal attorney in a death penalty case). At those moments we forget all the other roles we *routinely* perform, many of which are just as valued as the one that is on our mind at the moment.

What To Do: Identify your *routine* roles that have value to you.

Why To Do It: It will help you live a values-based life. When the going gets rough, you can remind yourself of all the things that you already do that are important.

How To Do It: Place a check mark on ten things from the following list that you value about yourself.

Motherhood	Complex	Strong
Fatherhood	Responsible	Incalcitrant
Neighborly	Friendly	Placid
Family Values	Distinguished	Welcoming

Spiritual	Irreverent	Obedient
Honest	Steady Job Holder	Feminine
Faithful	Sexy	Gainful
Clean	Tidy	Tall
Informed	Historian	Whimsical
Well Read	Disruptive	Steadfast
Kind	Loving	Colorful
Helpful	Shameful	Memorable
Diligent	Corrupt	Contained
Resourceful	Intellectual	Thrill Seeker
Conversational	Agreeable	Detailed
Emotional	Protective	Articulate
Sensitive	Sweet	Provider
Compassionate	Individualistic	Modest
Talented	Successful	Rational
Funny	Gleeful	Enjoyable
Rich	Communal	Suspicious
Moral	Predictable	Happy
Complicated	Hobo	Gregarious
Simple	Superior	Careful
Gorgeous	Gentle	Accepting
Vivid	Handsome	Regimented
Critical	Politically Correct	Agile
Thoughtful	Curvy	Popular
Well Mannered	Spontaneous	Solid
Pacific	Argumentative	Contrite
Rowdy	Breathtaking	Erudite
Mercurial	Jokester	Safe
Famous	Nasty	Narcissistic
Manipulative	Pretty	Authoritative
Masculine	Conniving	Genial
Incorrigible	Peaceful	Tender

Smart	Musical	Well spoken
Reserved	Good natured	Erratic
Structured	Short	Nonjudgmental
Powerful	Genial	Unpredictable
Understanding	Adonis-like	Have rhythm
Soft	Mild	Safe
Agreeable	Athletic	Indulgent
Fond	Listening	Yielding
Variegated	Polite	Admirable
Low keyed	Well preserved	Knowledgeable
Delicate	Esteemed	Svelte
Affectionate	Gracious	Tolerant
Virtuous	Secure	Adoring
Respected	Disobedient	Lenient

Do you see any themes on your checklist? Write them here. You will refer to them later.

Example: My highest values are about being respectful. Or, I tend to like to be a joker; I value having fun.

_____

_____

_____

_____

You can think of other qualities you have, or admire in others, to fully appreciate that we all have many attributes, roles, qualities, that help define and give words to our identity or our ideal identity we wish to create. Are we born with these virtues or deficits? Probably we learned them, some attributes "worked" for us and others did not.

We were modeled and influenced by our interpersonal environments. And we can always create or renew those we do not routinely use.

Narratives

The OED defines a narrative as "that narrates or recounts; occupied or concerned with, having the character of...a consecutively developed story...a history, tale, story, recital" (Vol. X, p. 220). So a narrative is a story, or a recounting of one. In psychology we refer to narratives as "life stories," or "scripts" that people follow to assist with the establishment of their identity (or a part of it). Your narrative can have a very beneficial function in your life if it is imbued with feelings, opinions, and beliefs that are positive, self-affirming, functional, and at least mostly accurate. On the other hand, if your self- narrative is punitive, self-effacing, leads to dysfunctional behavior, and leads to an underestimating of your abilities and talents, then your narrative needs to change.

Your self-narrative, even though a story or tale, is very much a part of your context and your sense of self. Note in the definition that a narrative is "occupied" and "concerned with." Looked at as a loosely-defined script, it can be predictive of your future behavior and feelings, coloring how you see both the world and your place in it.

Even a self-enhancing narrative may have aspects that lead to dysfunctional behavior. Think of someone you know or have read about that has such high self-esteem that they think traditional interpersonal rules should not apply to them. They can become careless towards others.

Example of Positive Narrative	Example of Negative Narrative
I was raised in a very loving family. My parents were considerate, giving, attentive, and always present when I needed them. We were not rich, but we always felt there was enough. We were encouraged to have friends, and to bring them over to the house. As a teenager, although there were typical conflicts, I was encouraged to make decisions on my own and to become a responsible adult. I try to be like my parents. Loving, attentive, skilled in the art of living life successfully, and treating others the way I was treated growing up.	My parents were ill-educated fools. They gave me so little in life as soon as I was old enough I ran away from home. I learned you can't trust others, and anything you get in life is full of effort and pain. It takes a lot for me to really trust anyone; they have to prove themselves to me. So I have few friends. My job stinks but it pays the bills and I'm independent. I don't have to rely on anyone. I don't understand why my kids hate me so, they should have seen the way I was treated (then maybe they would be thankful for what they have). Life is hard. You have to be tough to survive.

What To Do: Identify and write a short narrative that you think exemplifies a description of yourself, your life story, and the lessons you learned from it.

Why To Do It: Such self-reflection will assist you in identification of helpful and hurtful aspects of the scripts by which you live.

How To Do It: Using the examples above as a guide, summarize how your childhood molded your view of the world and your attitudes, beliefs, and broad values about living your life. Give this some thought.

Include in your narrative:

- Childhood experiences (general memories)
- Attitudes about yourself and others in broad general ways
- Your self image or self esteem (or lack thereof)

Write your narrative below:

_____

_____

_____

_____

_____

_____

_____

_____

_____

_____

What aspects from what you wrote do you like and approve of:

Examples:

Makes me feel good reading it.
Makes me appreciate of what I have. I feel fortunate.
I sure overcame some obstacles!
A good script to live by. I wish all others had such a script.

What I like from my narrative:

_____

_____

_____

_____

_____

What aspects from your narrative made you feel sad, disappointed, regretful, or angry?

Examples:

My father really had a bad influence on me, and I can see I am engaging in some of his bad habits.
I have a dismal view of life.

Makes me want to cry because I deserved better.

What I dislike from my narrative:

_____

_____

_____

_____

_____

_____

One of the aspects of a narrative or script is that it can often be predictive of one's future. Why? The narrative forms a holistic outlook towards life, influencing your threat assessments, your valuation of others' intentions toward you, whether you see opportunity for the future or obstacles, and can influence how you feel independent of what is going on in the moment. For example, in one study encouraging a feeling of gratitude and thankfulness lead to less materialism and greater generosity in the future (Chaplin et al, 2018). So your narrative can be changed. But first you must identify what aspects of your narrative are predictive of the future.

From our Examples of Positive and Negative Narratives above, predictive aspects would be:

From Positive Narrative Example Predictive Aspects	From Negative Narrative Example Predictive Aspects
• Sees world as friendly and loving, and will therefore venture out and form relationships • Encourages others to make own decisions and will not be restrictive or overbearing on others • Will not be over materialistic, will make do with what is available • Will have a positive outlook on self and life in general	• Sees the world as a dangerous place, and will be prone to identify possible threats before they occur • Will have a difficult time gaining or giving love • Will have conflict and disappointing relationship within own family in the future • Will experience grief, effortfulness, and disappointment frequently in the future • Will focus on independence and survival rather than happiness

Write what you can see as predictive from your own narrative:

_____

_____

_____

_____

_____

Thus far you have identified your narrative, assessed what you like and dislike about it, and determined how your narrative may help or harm you in the future. Now let's alter your narrative in ways that diminish the harmful and increase the helpful in your future. This is not an academic exercise, since how you see yourself and your situation greatly influences your behavior and feelings (both in the here-and-now and in the future). Let's take the negative narrative example (from pages 164 – 165) and alter it in order to potentially change the future probabilities:

Altered Negative Narrative
My parents were ill-educated, so I guess they didn't know any better. I ran and avoided situations that I felt were empty, and now I'm applying my effort at creating the kind of family and world I never had. I have difficulty trusting others, so I take time to give people the benefit of the doubt. Nobody has anything to prove to me, so I attempt to take people as they are and spend time with people who don't purposefully hurt me. I have an understanding that many relationship hurts are due to communication and being defensive. I'm trying to be less and less defensive on an everyday basis. I'm looking at my talents more and more and want to find a job I enjoy. Every time I think of "survival issues" in my head I'm consciously replacing it with "quality of life issues." I'm telling my children more than once a day how much I love them, even when they express anger towards me, It will be difficult but I'm strong and I can do it. I'm beginning to see life as a challenge rather than simply hard.

In this altered narrative the following objectives or goals are seen:

- Desire to avoid less
- Forgiveness

- Become less defensive
- Form relationships despite distrust
- Be mindful of how people *are* acting rather than how I expect them to be
- Goal for improving life situation (job)
- Improving family relationships
- Taking a more positive attitude

Write your altered narrative here:

_____

_____

_____

_____

_____

_____

_____

_____

_____

_____

_____

Periodically review your altered narrative and ask yourself:

- Recently what have I done to make my altered narrative *real*
- What obstacles must I overcome to make the altered narrative easier to accomplish?
- Are there ways I can change my environment to encourage my altered narrative?
- Have I been mindful of my successes?

ASSERTIVENESS

Sometimes we can't change our environment, but we have substantial control over ourselves. Most people choose not to divorce their spouse after an argument, to disinherit their children when they are disobedient, to quit their employment when they don't get their way, or to move residence after conflict with a neighbor. However, even within an existing context that is challenging you can alter your behavior to improve outcomes.

One such technique is assertiveness. Many of us have heard the basic principles: use a calm voice as you express your desires that may be contrary to the wishes of another, stand up for your rights or the rights of others rather than remain silent, passive behavior is ill advised since you forgo your wants, aggressive behavior may get you what you want but will eventually backfire because people will not want to be around you, and passive-aggressive behavior (avoiding direct confrontation but slyly expressing your displeasure, with such strategies as procrastination, misplacing important materials, verbalizing to everyone but the person you are concerned with how disapproving you are of them, or otherwise thwarting someone's intentions behind the scenes).

Here are some examples of the three types of behavior:

Passive Behaviors (Not Good)	Assertive Behaviors (Good)	Aggressive Behaviors (Not Good)
• Telling somebody yes or okay and then taking an unnecessary amount of time doing it • "I'm okay with whatever you want to do," when you really are not • Keeping silent when someone does something that makes you angry	• Calmly telling someone no • "I would rather do it this way rather than the way you suggested." • Calmly telling the person they have angered you	• Yelling at someone for having asked you the request • Belittle the requestor for having made the request • Name calling, put-downs, humiliation, threats

Here is a graphic illustration.

Assertiveness Dimensions or Domains

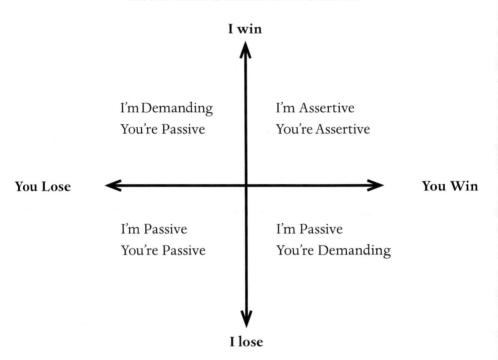

Passive OR Aggressive Situation From the Past	How I Wish To Be Assertive In the Future
My mother came over and told me how I should be treating my children, and I told her to mind her own business, that she herself was a crappy mother and had no right to tell me anything about childrearing. All this was shouting at her.	The next time mom comments on my parenting I want to remain calm and tell her that she should understand that parenting styles differ, and I prefer she not comment on mine.

Similarly, identify situations from the past where you want to practice assertion.

Passive OR Aggressive Situation From the Past	How I Wish To Be Assertive In the Future
_____	_____
_____	_____
_____	_____
_____	_____
_____	_____
_____	_____
_____	_____
_____	_____
_____	_____
_____	_____
_____	_____
_____	_____
_____	_____
_____	_____
_____	_____
_____	_____
_____	_____

There are many books and workbooks on assertion. I like the brief and informative *Your Perfect Right* (Alberti & Emmons, 1985).

Weave It Together

We began this chapter with a definition of "context" as a weaving together of a connected structure. The structure in this case is psychological. The building blocks of this psychological structure are family/relationships, culture, neighborhood, job, the narratives you have created about yourself (or accepted from others), and the many roles you play. Your "self" is your identity and nature, and both are in constant flux based upon both your context and your values.

Look back on your responses to the exercises from page 150 to 159. Regardless of your rankings at the time, looking in retrospect, rank order the following domains from 1 (most influential) to 5 (lease influential):

      _____Family
      _____Culture
      _____Religious/Spiritual
      _____Neighborhood
      _____Job
      _____Roles

Now compare those results to your qualities (pages xxx to xxx) you endorsed? Do you notice any patterns? If all of your identity qualities were about softness (spirituality, helpful, emotional, sensitive, loving, sweet, gracious, tolerant, tender, etc.) but your main context is job where you serve in marketing in an ever challenging and almost cut-throat environment, then maybe something is wrong that needs correcting.

Likewise, if your preferred context value is family but your identity qualities are mostly about respect (informed, diligent, regimented, powerful, structured, etc.) then there is a mismatch there. Your identified personal qualities do not maximize the probability that your family is going to feel safe and loved by you. They will perhaps feel economically secure that you will provide a roof over their head, but what about their emotional needs?

Or the person who really prefers to be soft but is in a competitive work environment full of need for "hard" not "soft"; think of the incongruence between the environment that is suited to you and the one you landed up in!

Should you "fight" your values? No. If your personality disposition and values are strongly in one direction (expressive, accepting, loving) it would be a strain for you to be a harsh disciplinarian with your children, to perform cold-call marketing with people who will be rude and disrespectful to your interruptions, or to draw lines in the sand during an interpersonal conflict that is unimportant to you because "somebody said I should." On the other hand, if your culture, personality, and values are for independent, strong and forceful, and you prefer decisive methods, it would be a strain for you to be tolerant and forgiving in your parenting style when you see transgressions. You might be great at marketing, business negotiating, and enforcing agreements already made.

BONDING AND INTERPERSONAL CONTEXTS

Most conflict occurs within social contexts (they want something different than what you want). Family settings are important contexts (Thompson, 2014). The probability of high conflict (with resulting strong emotions) is greater in intimate relationships than elsewhere. We expect more from those we love than we do strangers, acquaintances, neighbors, or coworkers. When we don't get what we want, we feel badly disappointed, and perhaps as much as furious.

Bonding (Bowlby, 1988) with others is a critical thing. Unbonded individuals are described as having an "attachment disorder." The inability to form secure bonds creates distress, mostly for those who want to love them. Bonding is the foundation of love, empathy for others, the ability to thrive as infants, and unfortunately also describes why some people are violent and stay in abusive relationships.

These issues are more than academic. They many times predict the future. Consider infancy. In Figure 12 below the infant in the moment is satisfied, sleeping. Then the infant soils his or her diaper, causing irritation. The baby cries in discomfort. The consoling mother changes the diaper, says soothing things to his/her child in a tone of voice that is reassuring and understood (whispering, with a different tone of voice than what you would use with another adult), and the child settles down. The bottom axis represents time and state of emotionality, while the vertical axis represents level of distress. Look at the following diagram and let's explore what it means.

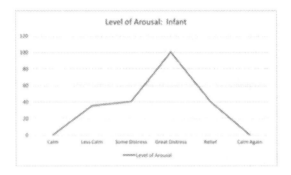

Figure 11: Emotional Arousal and Bonding in Infancy

First the infant is asleep and satisfied, then soils the diaper, over time the soiled diaper causes great distress. The mother changes the diaper and it brings immediate relief. The soothing voice and action (including touch) brings the infant back to normal. Repeated experiences of this tension and tension-relief is the basis of bonding. The infant "knows" that mama brings relief from discomfort.

This template about bonding applies not only to infants, but to adults as well. I understand that many (maybe most) people say that sex is not the most important aspect of a relationship. I agree. However, sexual intimacy is yet another example of the important role of bonding (that is a conditioned, repeated, and satisfying experience that most desire to repeat again and again). The same pattern as with the infant: you are satisfied (calm). Yet you become less calm as time goes on. You eventually feel sexually needy. While we probably would not describe it as great distress, sexual tension and need for release is high. You have intimacy, and with the orgasm (or just the intimacy of touching and mutuality) brings immediate relief and the sexual tension is rapidly diminished,

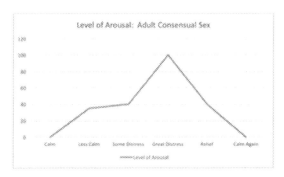

Figure 12: Emotional Arousal in Adult Intimacy

This is yet another component of bonding that acts as a buffer against later extraneous conflicts (like chores, money, statements made, etc.). You stay in the relationship not just because it is convenient or the good outweighs the bad, but because of that emotional bond as well.

Let's take another example to show how robust this understanding of the bonding process can be. With domestic or family violence the same pattern can be seen. Everything is right with the world in the beginning, but gradually someone begins to annoy you (perhaps in the beginning with trivial things: "will you pick up after yourself," "turn that TV down!," "shut your mouth, I'm watching this program." You or them become irritated, and the irritation builds. Then the physical assault occurs (a slap, a push, a punch in the face). The aggressor immediately becomes apologetic (perhaps afraid that you will leave, that you will call the police, or you will call your big muscular brother who will come over and pulverize them). They say they are sorry. They hug you, they kiss you, they say it will never happen again. Maybe they show affection so infrequently that this "hearts and flowers" stage feels great. They may ask for sex. Your anxiety (arousal, tension, irritation) lowers, and the bond is strengthened. You stay in the abusive relationship.

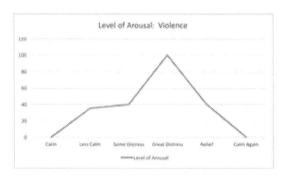

Figure 13: Emotional Arousal in the Cycle of Violence

You may assume that it is women who are the victims and men are the perpetuators, and many times this is correct. However, I have seen many examples where it is the woman who slaps the man's face, throws a telephone or wine glass in his face, or literally stabs him in the back.

One resource on domestic violence that may be helpful is a book by Roberson and Wallace (2016). In my 40 years of clinical practice I always recommended to my patients that they call 911 for the police immediately when violence occurs. A night in jail can be a sobering experience for someone who has not learned that violence is *wrong*. The excuse that "they made me do it" is wrong. Having a reason to physically attack someone is rarely an excuse. The only exception I can think of is when you are defending yourself against an immediate sexual or physical attack.

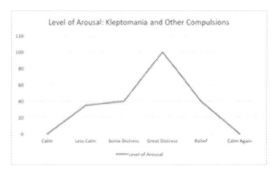

Figure 14: Kleptomania and Other Emotional Compulsions

Kleptomania is a recurrent urge to steal, typically without regard for need or profit.

It is different from being a thief, burglar, swindler or cheater because in those cases the person "takes" due to profit. "Why did you rob the bank?" "Because they had the money I needed." A kleptomaniac has another purpose, rather than profit they want to see if they can get away with it without getting caught. It is an excellent example of thrill seeking, arousal reduction, and an ill-formulated method to feel satisfied and discharge their tension.

So let's follow a hypothetical kleptomaniac. They are sitting at home calm and watching a movie on Netflix. They are initially calm, but the movie they are watching does not capture their interest. They begin to think about the last time they stole something (less calm stage), and distraction does not work. They think about the security methods stores employ are lousy (some distress). They get up and go to Macy's. They look around, and decide to take a wallet (great distress). They walk out of the store and throw the wallet in the trash can outside of Macy's (relief stage). They go back home and continue to watch the Netflix movie they had abandoned (calm again stage).

I use the example of kleptomania because it is a rare disorder (most readers don't have it). As a result there are fewer defenses against it (I don't have it, so why worry?). But think about the many other dynamics that follow the same pattern of addiction: alcoholism, drug abuse, gambling or betting, sexual addictions, food addictions, or cheating on school tests. There are many situations where the dynamics outlined above apply. Sometimes if we know we are engaging in a "bad" behavior pattern we rationalize or deny it. Whenever you see someone engaged in a destructive behavior pattern ask yourself "Are there ways in which I too engage in something different, but as a similar process?

If you find yourself in repetitive situations that even you yourself disapprove, ask yourself if you are engaging in this destructive "attachment" process.

What To Do: Identify at least one destructive behavior pattern you have perhaps related to attachment.

Why To Do It: See your "blind spots." Have plans to change unwanted behavior and the feelings that result from them.

How To Do It: Think of situations where you said to yourself, immediately after doing something that you are not proud of, "Wow, I feel much better now."

Example:

Topic	Behavior	Plans To Do Differently

Beer	Felt sad for myself last night, consumed two six-packs of beer in one night.	Next time I'm sad I'll call a friend who is supportive rather than argumentative, or watch a comedy movie on Netflix, or do deep breathing exercises, or body scan, or go to the gym and work out.

Topic	Behavior	Plans To Do Differently

Taking context and self in to consideration in your decision-making and coping is thus important. Implied in all of the above is that some of us have a rigid view of "self" because we do not take in to account the myriad of factors that makes us who we are. And if we begin to tease apart the components, we may reassess our sense of self and the context that laid the groundwork for it. This can be a very productive, if difficult, process. Awareness of the map we are using may make us think about the frustrations in obtaining our goals; maybe you use the wrong map. Perhaps you are using the roadmap (how to get from point A to Point B) when you should be using the aerial map (taking the big picture, as in evaluating the difference between short-term and long-term goals—not seeing the forest due to the trees).

Our maps are "schemas" (a lens view of how to view the world; a model or outline). You have in this chapter examined some of the main schemas we use to define our sense of self. Re-evaluating their importance and validity to you (rather than being on automatic pilot from what you developed over time unconsciously) can improve your emotional coping strategies. The major domains of context and self (you may think of others important to you) reviewed in this chapter include:

- Family
- Neighborhood
- Culture
- Nationality
- Spiritual and Religious
- Acceptance and tolerance for differences (or not)
- Job
- Roles you perform
- Bonding and biological conditioning ("automatic" emotional responses)
- Addictions and how they are influenced by biological factors

THE PATH OF WISDOM

To be told that you are wise is one of the highest compliments you can receive. Surely to be told that you are a good person, moral, decisive, knowledgeable, industrious, hard-working, kind, or loving are all welcomed compliments as well. Yet they do not rise to the level of wisdom. Other compliments or attributes speak to a single dimension of human character, yet wisdom speaks to a set of qualities that combine and weave each characteristic in to a mosaic that defines use of your knowledge and feelings in both practical and abstract ways.

A wise person knows when to speak, and when to be silent. Wisdom brings confidence of when to act, and when to wait. Wisdom demands thought and action that fosters the common good, not just your own. Wisdom is loving and kind, but also practical and functional given context. Wisdom is self-knowledge as well as astute understanding of others. Wisdom is about attending to both broad ideals as well as mundane facts. Wisdom is more than practical (doing "what works"), it is also about reflection, meditating about 'right' and 'wrong' but proceeding on the path of righteousness without civil disobedience or hate, fear, or anger.

Let's look at how the OED (Vol. XX, 2001) defines the following terms:

> **Wisdom** (1) capacity of judging rightly in matters relating to life and conduct; soundness of judgment in the choice of means and ends; sometimes, less strictly, sound sense. Especially in practical affairs; opposite to folly.
>
> (2) Knowledge (especially of a high or obtuse kind; enlightenment, learning, or erudition; also practical knowledge, or understanding, expert in an art (page 421).
>
> **Wise** Manner, mode, fashion, style especially habitual manner of action, habit, custom. Having or exercising sound judgment or discernment; capable of judging truly what is right or fitting, and disposed to act accordingly; having the ability to perceive and adopt the best means for accomplishing an end; characterized by good sense and prudence (page 423).

Having practical understanding and ability; skillful, cleaver, skilled, expert.

Having knowledge, well informed, instructed (p. 424).

So wisdom is about the fundamental pragmatics of life but also about the recognition and management of uncertainty (Baltes & Staudinger, 2000). Uncertainty and ambiguity deserve further comment. You would not consider someone wise who felt they had all the facts and did not want to be bothered with more, and was willing to courageously go forward in spite of contrary evidence.

We would call this folly rather than wisdom. Yet much of life is ambiguous, not neatly categorized as good or bad, or right or wrong.

Examples could include the following kinds of situations and questions:

- Should I take this class because I find it very interesting, even though it does not meet my major requirements for graduation?
- Should I get divorced from my spouse due to the daily frustration and agony it brings me, even though it means my children will be raised in a broken home and the economics of it will be very difficult?
- Do I want to "take the high road" with my brother who exposes what I see as constant ill-informed beliefs and attitudes, and keep quiet and not reinforce his incessant chatter?
- Should I begin attending other church services, even though I have been disappointed that the parishioner's do not consistently or even partially follow the belief systems exposed by the church?
- Shall I divest my interests in politics because I see so much corruption?
- Shall I follow my feelings to disengage from this or that, or follow my thoughts that these are important and meaningful activities to pursue?

Wisdom has been studied mostly by philosophy and religious studies, but also by cultural anthropology, political science, education, and psychology (Baltes & Staudinger, 2000). We have also seen it applied in business (Tusinska, 2019). Major religious/meditative approaches focus on wisdom rather than salvation (Tusinka, 2019), and research on emotion and motivation have defined wisdom as "to live in the present, plan for the future, and profit from the past"

(Gasper & Bramesfeld, 2006). We have even seen it applied in dental practice (Apfel, 2015).

Wisdom addresses the "means versus the ends" conflict. With wisdom you do not suffer casualties for a just cause. Instead you determine other less harmful means to obtain your end. Even if the casualties are that another's esteem and self-respect are threatened by your cause, you elect other less harmful means to obtain your objective. In a political situation you might attend or give lectures, participate or organize a peaceful rally, vote people out of office with whom you disagree, or gather the attention of local news stations to air your views.

In an interpersonal situation you might divert attention to another topic by asking questions which change the topic, you might yourself change the topic of conversation, you begin a remembrance of a new topic that is related but detours the conversation ("You remember when Aunt Agnes …"), or you look at them blankly to quietly communicate your disinterest. In an intrapersonal situation (your own thoughts and feelings), you use distraction (engage action on an irrelevant content), be mindful of the conflict then move to valuation (how important is this to me, really?), you reappraise the prompters that promote the thoughts or feelings, and you use self-compassionate self-statements to resolve the conflict.

Wisdom is more than knowledge (a set of facts, no matter how skilled or practiced), more than folk knowledge (the armchair version of what other's do and say), the ability to identify problems well, or giving advice. Wisdom is the weaving together of these concepts and more.

The Role of Ambiguity

I was the President of the Student Body at the College of the Pacific, a school of the University of the Pacific. I told one of the

Deans, Ken Beauchamp: "You know the most frequent concern I hear from students here? That in spite of the excessively high tuition we pay, we are not being prepared to get a good paying job!" Dr. Beauchamp paused for only a brief second and replied, "The purpose of a liberal arts education is not to prepare you for a job, but to prepare you for life." I answered, likewise without hesitation, "What does that mean?" He replied, "The liberal arts provide a tolerance for ambiguity, and a new way to view the experiences of life."

I had to ponder this conversation, because it has stuck with me for forty years. In almost all my classes the professor would begin with "this is what we know" and at the end of the class conclude with an even longer list of "what we don't know." The more you know about a certain topic, the more you come to realize the unanswered questions and new facts to arise, how historically we were asking the wrong questions, and how other disciplines (with a different set of lenses through which to view the world) shed light on the same topic or phenomenon.

It is no different with the individual. You may think you know Kevin quite well. But then Kevin behaves inconsistently with how you would expect him to act. You had not explored all there is to know about Kevin, and there is ambiguity (not being able to see it all because there are blind spots or mercurial aspects of the person-situation context).

What does "tolerating" ambiguity mean? You understand there are hidden dark waters to every situation and context. You expect there are issues you have not considered. You accept the limits of your knowledge. You appreciate that your value system may be different from other individuals, other cultures, and other contexts. You invite yourself to have new and different perspectives without sacrificing your own values. Or more deeply, you are willing to reappraise your values given more context, more information, and more experience.

Dimensions of Wisdom

As you can see from the above, by embracing the notion of ambiguity, not all the dimensions of wisdom can be delineated. There may be more, many more, than the ones presented in the wisdom literature (Baltes & Staudinger, 2000) and elsewhere. Here are a few I came up with:

Dimensions or Domains of Wisdom

- Having life goals, and weighing them within context
- Having integrity (saying and doing what you know to be true; being consistent)
- All life is relative (my goals are different than yours, and my goals may change)
- Value-Driven: action or behavior devoid of a value is less important
- Understanding context (situational demands are different from values and goals)
- Understanding self (your identity is more than the situation and the context)
- Feelings are transitory (they come and go)
- Words describe more than they define ("the map is not the territory")
- Uncertainty is one of the few immutable facts of life (along with death and taxes)
- Your attention to the environment is extremely limited (we don't have all the facts)
- A sense of community (we are all in this boat together, although all different)
- A sense of the common good (individualism vs. community)
- A sense of commonality (we share more in common than we are different)

- A sense of autonomy (responsibility for one's own actions, and the power that comes with that)
- Practicality is valued
- Judicious expression (knowing when to speak and when to be quiet)
- Judicious advice-giving (listen, evaluate, and advise with good intentions)
- Judicious action (when to identify problems and fix them, and when to ignore them)
- Respect (for fellow mankind, the environment, and culture)
- Respectful behavior (enacting respect in outward verbal and behavioral ways)
- Adherence to the principle of relativism (values, cultures, situations, and views change)
- Avoidance of rigidity (in thought, behavior, identities, and values)
- Watchful of language and how it can inflame or diminish conflict
- Compassionate (both to self and others)
- Observing with fresh and watchful views of self and the others (mindfulness)
- Openness to experience (not rejecting experience but welcoming it)
- Do no harm
- Recognize the existence of suffering within self and others
- Avoiding exploitation of others and self
- Belief in shared prosperity (giving more than taking)
- Meaning is valued above practicality

There are many hurdles in living your life with wisdom. Foremost among them are asking the right questions (Gasper & Bramesfeld, 2006). You have all probably heard the parable of the three blind men feeling the elephant and attempting to describe it. One focuses on the trunk, the other the torso, the other the ears. They all come to different conclusions about how to define the elephant. So what is the right question? There is no necessary answer, because knowing the right question begs the answer. The answer depends on the context, the question itself, and the purpose of the question. And the parable itself is instructive: why ask blind men to describe what a sighted man can see with his own eyes? We are mostly in the same situation as the blind men when asked to be wise when we perhaps do not have all the resources to *be* wise.

And wisdom changes with the passage of time, your lifespan. It is wise to have fun between periods of instruction as a youth (it refreshes, brings perspective, increases attentiveness, and embellishes life itself). In older ages reflection rather than activity replaces fun. Study after study have shown this age-related or developmental phenomenon (Erikson, 1982).

Here is what Erikson proposed in terms of stages of development over time:

Stage	Psychosocial Crisis	Basic Virtue	Age
1.	Trust vs. Mistrust	Hope	0 - 1½
2.	Autonomy vs. Shame	Will	1½ - 3
3.	Initiative vs. Guilt	Purpose	3 - 5
4.	Industry vs. Inferiority	Competency	5 - 12
5.	Identity vs. Role Confusion	Fidelity	12 - 18
6.	Intimacy vs. Isolation	Love	18 - 40
7.	Generativity vs. Stagnation	Care	40 - 65
8.	Ego Integrity vs. Despair	Wisdom	65+

In Erickson's view you had to master one level of accomplishment or your ability to complete the next was impaired. Wisdom was not reached until you learned hope, developed will, purpose, competency, fidelity in your identity (that did not occur until you were 18), learned to love another (note the high range he proposes, from the age of 18 until 40!), what he calls care (being able to contribute your accumulated knowledge to others), and then only in very old age are you capable of wisdom. Let's hope he was wrong and that wisdom can be cultivated throughout the lifespan. Nevertheless, his model does inform us that wisdom is not something easy to accomplish, and in his lens view of the world it is a lifelong task toward which we strive.

Interestingly, some more modern research confirms Erikson's notion that wisdom, or the ability to effectively engage in emotion regulation, improves with age (Charles & Carstensen, 2014). The elder focus on positive memories rather than negative ones, and focus on the positive in the here-and-now rather than the negative.

Although I do not believe that the wisdom process can be broken down in to a flow chart, let's examine just two aspects challenging our ability to use wisdom (arousal and meaning).

As we've discussed previously, arousal or high emotionality can lead to impulsivity, poor decision making, and poor outcomes. Does this mean feeling deeply and strongly is bad? No, it means that when you are passionate and excited and act quickly you may be disappointed. For a positive example, imagine the man of your dreams proposes marriage. Do you stop and ask yourself questions: How long have I known this guy? What are his values? Does he want to have kids? Does his family share the same values I have? Is he from the same culture? What does he expect in a wife different from what he expected in a girlfriend? Has he ever in his life been in jail? Can he keep a job? Have I seen his behavior in settings outside of a date? If you have reviewed, even dreamed about all these questions, and you still waited for his commitment of marriage—very good! The following figure is designed to get you to ask generic questions about any situation you confront where perhaps you are not so certain how to proceed.

High Emotions or Arousal

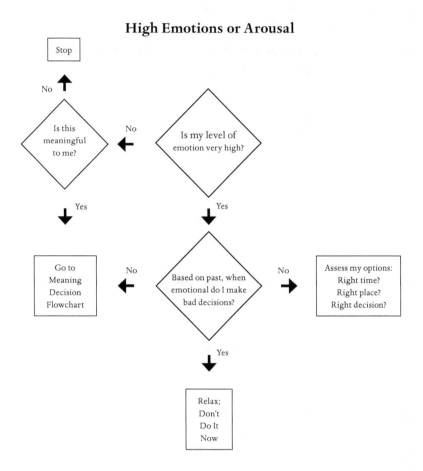

As Freud (1930) said, "It is not easy to deal scientifically with feelings" (p. 65, *Civilization and Its Discontents*). In addition to high emotionality (as above), another factor that can preclude the use of wisdom is your ability to identify meaning to you. This may sound strange, in that everyone should know what is meaningful to them, but you may not take that domain or factor in to your decision making. Look at the following flowchart (start on the right side of the chart:

Meaning Decision-Making Flowchart

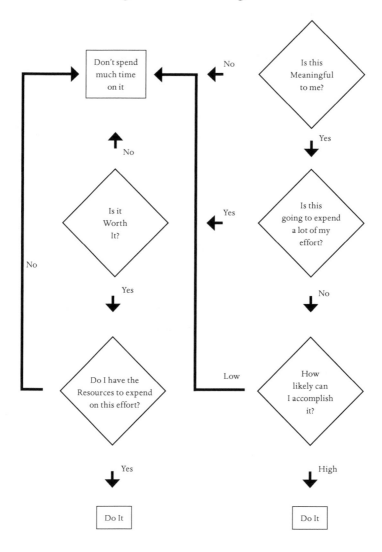

So there is no formula to the path of wisdom, just a few guideposts.

In terms of behavior, ask yourself if the behavior makes good feelings linger and bad feelings fade. Does the behavior serve important values and roles (context) in your life?

In terms of feelings, do the feelings support the kind of life and lifestyle you value? Examine the prompters for the feelings, and decrease the negative ones and optimize the positive ones.

Community is an important feature for both happiness and longevity. Are you engaging in activities that bring you closer to important others? Do you feel you 'belong' in some contexts and some groups? Remember a community can be your family, your church, your neighborhood, or your organizations. Think of the concept of community broadly.

Are the strategies you use effortful or easy? Are the effortful ones worth it (do they "pay off")? Are the easy ones worth it (do they "pay off")?

Continue your path to wisdom by weaving together all the concepts in this workbook, and practicing them frequently. Use the extra worksheets in the Appendix for your work. Feel pride that you know yourself better, your context better, have more confidence in your decision-making process, and feel less threat and more security.

Emotion regulation can be more than making good feelings linger and bad feelings fade. It can increase your ability to follow the path of wisdom.

10
REVIEW

Why a review? Mood management requires practice, and practice means remembering and working through the many principles in this workbook. In the first introductory chapter we learned that both general and emotional problem solving involves a strategy. We also learned that human suffering need not have a formal diagnosis. Many of us have difficulties in life that can benefit from these robust techniques even if we are simply sad and not depressed, simply unfulfilled and not anxious, and want improvement even when things go well. There does not have to be something "wrong" with you in order to want to feel even better. In the second chapter we saw that there is great scientific evidence to support the approaches suggested in this book.

In the third chapter we learned that the practice of mindfulness is powerful. Sounds simple, but it is hard to do. It is hard to do precisely because mindfulness of experience has been trained out of us, unintentionally and without malice. And it is difficult to regain. With mindfulness practice we regain self-control, flexibility, improve our concentration and attention, regain acceptance, decrease emotional and cognitive reactivity, and even improve our physical health.

Next we review the biopsychosocial model of emotions. It predicts that much of what we see as a threat can be modified. It is modified by the experience itself reappraised and changed: our body, thoughts, genetic background, social experience, values and meanings, and situational factors are all modifiable to some extent.

Then comes the "meat" of this book. Lots of people feel happy, so how come many times I am not? I want it. I want to feel happy. Others have it more than me, it seems. Sometimes we don't "have it" because we feel we don't deserve it. We find reasons, many of them, not to have it. You are invited to request three critical factors in to your life: inspiration, meaning, and vivid experiences. These are not necessarily religious (although they can be), socially approved (although they can be), or even in conscious awareness (although they, too, can be). Feeling good is about experiences: real/imagined/projected/planned. Some experiences we've never tried, and we should. Some experiences we rarely do, but could. Sometimes we choose not to have new or different experiences because of the perceived cost of doing so. Sometimes we never connected the dots between feeling good on purpose; wishing we could stumble upon happiness rather than having to make it happen.

Specific strategies to feel good, and make it frequent and "stick" are reviewed: rekindle, vicarious, and reappraisal tools are given.

In most of chapter 6 I deal with how to not feel bad so often. Pain and discomfort are a part of life. None of us can always avoid emotional pain, but neither do we have to prolong it. Some strategies rarely, or never, work. Like denial. The workbook helps us to identify denial, as a central culprit in sustaining misery. Avoidance is more complicated issue because sometimes to avoid is good and sometimes it is bad. This workbook tries to help you decide which kind (good or bad) you use,

Then we get to a pernicious (and unfortunately pervasive) theme of this workbook: perception. Thoughts (beliefs) can be real or imagined.

Truthful or downright distorted. This workbook attempts to help you discriminate between the two. Other enemies in prolonging unwanted feelings (procrastination, delayed and destructive body sensations, and impatience) are reviewed and alternatives (good problem solving—pain relieving strategies) are given.

In chapter 8 issues of Context and Self are explored. Frequently (almost always) these issues are ignored or watered down in self-help workbooks (especially in cognitive-behavioral workbooks, that can be especially useful). Why? Like the following chapter, issues about identity and context are so complicated that it is difficult to break down in to component units. It is not so much that professionals think it is unimportant, but because it is so broad and less researched no one wants to deal with it. To me it is like saying "let's wait until the jury comes in." Well, the context defines values, and values define meaning. Explore it. Perhaps you see issues of family, neighborhood (broadly defined), culture, religion, employment/job, and roles or reference groups differently than most. Those issues nevertheless influence you and your feelings perhaps more than you thought.

Equally important is the role of narratives. What is your life story? A life story is the story **you** tell, even if only to yourself in your own mind. We watch television, movies, biographies...they all tell a story. Sometimes fortunately, and sometimes unfortunately, the narrative we have about our life is a script (and we live by it thoughtlessly, like an actor in a play rather than a human being who has choice and can change the script if the outcomes are not wanted.

Finally, decreasing unwanted feelings has to do with tolerance. Yuk. And worse, but similar yuk, acceptance. Tolerance and acceptance, such easy words to say, and so difficult to practice. Especially in American culture our emphasis is on changing things we don't like. But some feelings are real and meant to be. They are not wrong. And some feelings that are unwanted can't be changed. Tolerance and acceptance are skills effective people have to master in order to decrease misery.

Chapter 9, The Path to Wisdom. Wisdom—does anyone have a path to it? I read and researched what philosophers, theologians, and even psychologists had to say about it. Sometimes a wise person keeps their mouth shut. That seems wise to me. Sometimes a wise person takes action. That too, seems wise. Knowing when to speak and when to be silent, when to act and when to be passive, when to advise and when to let events unfold without your intervention at all, is a murky set of alternatives.

Yet most of recognize when someone gives us wise advice. When we feel strongly about something and someone cautions us to relax, not be impetuous, to "sleep on it," we simply know that they are right (even if we don't like it). Understanding ambiguity, that not everything is black or white, that meaning mostly is contextual and transient, makes life more complex but reflects reality (or our best perception of that) more understandable.

The polemics of ambiguity both define how to be wise as well as why it is difficult to define at all: practical vs. idealistic, values vs. practicality, respect vs. rebellion, abandonment of self vs. preserving self, fluidity of strategies vs. familiarity of strategies, and maturity vs. freshness. Wisdom is something that is aspirational and toward which all of us must strive.

∞

Practice the workbook skills receptively, and notice the difference in your feelings, by completing the additional worksheets that follow..

References

Adele, M. H., & Feldman, G. (2004). Clarifying the Construct of Mindfulness in the Context of Emotion Regulation and the Process of Change in Therapy. *Clinical Psychology*, 11, pp. 255–262.

Alberta, R. & Emmons, M. (1985) *Your Perfect Right* 10th Edition. Oakland: Impact Publishers (now New Harbinger Press).

Anderson, N., & Estee, S. (2002). Medical Cost Offsets Associated with Health Care: A Brief Review. *Department of Health and Human Services Research and Data Analysis Division*, 3, 28.

Apfel, S. (2015). Wisdom. *The New York State Dental Journal*, 81 (5), pp. 20–30.

Baltes, P. B., & Staudinger, U. M. (2000). Wisdom: A Metaheuristic (Pragmatic) to Orchestrate Mind and Virtue Toward Excellence. *American Psychologist*, (55) 1, pp. 122–136.

Berking, M., & Schwartz, J. (2014). Affect Regulation Training in Gross, James J. *Handbook of Emotion Regulation, Second Edition*. New York: Guilford Press.

Bishop, S. R., Lau, M.A., Shapiro, S. L., Carlson, L., Anderson, N. D., & Devins, G. (2004). Mindfulness: A Proposed Operational Definition. *Clinical Psychology*, 11, pp. 230–241.

Bowlby, J. (1988). *A Secure Base*. Abingdon-on-Thames, UK: Routledge.

Brown, K. W., Ryan, R. M., & Creswell, J. D. (2007). Mindfulness: Theoretical Foundations and Evidence for its Salutary Effects. *Psychological Inquiry*, 18, pp. 211–137.

Burns, D. D. (1980). *Feeling Good: The New Mood Therapy*. New York: Harper Collins.

Cahn, B. R., & Polich, J. (2009). Meditation (Vipassana) and the P3a Event-Related Brain Potential. *International Journal of Psychophysiology*, 72, pp. 51-60.

Chambers, R., Lo, B. C. Y., & Allen, N. B. (2008). The Impact of Intensive Mindfulness Training on Attentional Control, Cognitive Style, and Affect. *Cognitive Therapy and Research*, 32, pp. 303–322.

Chaplin, L., John, D, Rindfleisch, A., & Froh, J. (2018). The impact of gratitude on adolescent materialism and generosity. The Journal of Positive Psychology. 14. 1-10.

Charles, S. K., & Carstensen, L. L. (2014). Emotion Regulation and Aging, in Gross, James J. *Handbook of Emotion Regulation, Second Edition*. New York: Guilford Press.

Cohen, S., Tyrrell, D.A.J., & Smith, A. P. (1993). Negative Life Events, Perceived Stress, Negative Affect, and Susceptibility to the Common Cold. *Journal of Personality and Social Psychology*, 64, pp. 131–140.

Corcoran, K. M., Farb, N., Anderson, A., & Segal, Z. V. (2010). Mindfulness and Emotion Regulation: Outcomes and Possible Mediating Mechanisms in A. M. Kring and D. M. Sloan *Emotion Regulation and Psychopathology: A Transdiagnostic Approach to Etiology and Treatment*. New York: Guilford Press, pp. 339–355.

Davidson, R. J., Kabat-Zinn, J., Schumacher, J., Rosenkranz, M., Muller, D., Santorelli, S. F., & Sheridan, J. F. (2003). Alteration in Brain an Immune Function Produced in Mindfulness Meditation. *Psychosomatic Medicine*, 66, pp. 149-152.

Davis, D. M., & Hayes, J. A. (2011). What Are the Benefits of Mindfulness? A Practice Review of Psychotherapy-Related Research. *Psychotherapy* (48), 2, pp. 198-208.

Dell'Orso, L., & Pini, Stefano. (2012). What Did We Learn From Research on Comorbidity in Psychiatry? Advantages and Limitations in the Forthcoming DSM-V Era. *Clinical Practice & Epidemiology in Mental Health*, 8, pp. 180–184.

DeSteno, D., Gross, J., & Kubzansky, L. (2013). Affective Science and Health: The Importance of Emotions and Emotion Regulation. *Health Psychology* (32), 5, pp. 474–486.

Erikson E. H. (1982). ***The life cycle completed***. New York: Norton.

Farb, N. A., Anderson, A. K., Irving, J. A. & Segel, Z. V. (2014). Mindfulness Interventions and Emotion Regulation, in Gross, James J. *Handbook of Emotion Regulation, Second Edition*. New York: Guilford Press.

Farb, N. A. S., Anderson, A. K., Mayberg, H., Bean, J., McKeon, D., & Segal, Z. V. (2010). Minding One's Emotions: Mindfulness Training Alters the Neural Expression of Sadness. *Emotion*, 10, pp. 25–33.

Fresco, D.M., Segal, Z. V., & Buis, Kennedy S. (2007). Relationship of Posttreatment Decentering and Cognitive Reactivity to Relapse in Major Depression. *Journal of Consulting and Clinical Psychology*, 75, pp. 447–455.

Freud, S. (1963) *Introductory Lectures on Psychoanalysis*. London: Hogarth Press. Originally published in 1915–1916.

Freud, S. Three Essays on the Theory of Sexuality. Hogarth Press: London, 1963. Originally published in 1905.

Freud, S. (1963). *Civilization and Its Discontents*. Hogarth Press: London, 1963. Originally published in 1930.

Fulton, P. R. Mindfulness as Clinical Training, in C. K. Germer, R. D., Siegel & P. R. Fulton (2005). *Mindfulness and Psychotherapy*. New York: Guilford Press, pp. 55–72.

Gaito, J. (1974). The Kindling Effect. *Physiological Psychology*, (2) 1, pp. 45-50.

Garland, E. L., Hanley, A. W., Goldin, P. R., & Gross, J. J. (2017). Testing the Mindfulness-to-Meaning Theory: Evidence for Mindful Positive Emotion Regulation from a Reanalysis of Longitudinal Data. *PLoS ONE* 12(12): e0187727.

Gasper, K., & Bramesfeld, K. D. (2006). Imparting Wisdom: Magda Arnold's Contribution to Research on Emotion and Motivation. *Cognition and Emotion*, (20) 7.

Gross, J. J. (2014). *Handbook of Emotion Regulation, Second Edition*. New York: Guilford Press.

Hanes, S. G., Feinleib, M., & Kannel, W. B. (1980). The Relationship of Psychosocial Factors to Coronary Heart Disease in the Farmington Study: III. Eight Year Incidence of Coronary Heart Disease. *American Journal of Epidemiology*, 111, pp. 37–58.

Haines, S. G., Gleeson, J., Kuppens, P., Hollenstein, T., Ciarrochi, J., Labuschagne, I., Grace, C. & Koval, P. (2016). The Wisdom to Know the Difference: Strategy-Situation Fit in Emotion Regulation in Daily Life Is Associated With Well-Being. *Psychological Science*, 27 (12), pp. 161–1659.

Hayakawa, S. I. & Hayakawa, A. R. (1991). *Language in Thought and Action*. New York: Houghton Mifflin Harcourt.

Healthwise. (2018). University of Michigan Health System. Online, Uofmhealth.org.

Hoffman, S. G., Grossman, P., & Hinton, D. E. (2011). Loving-kindness and compassion meditation: Potential for Psychological Interventions. *Clinical Psychology Review*, 31(7), pp. 1126–1132.

Hoskin, M. (1999). The Cambridge Concise History of Astronomy. New York: Cambridge University Press.

Huta, V. (2016). *An Overview of Hedonic and Eudaimonic Well Being Concepts, in Handbook of Media Use and Well-Being*. Abingdon-on-Thames, UK: Routledge.

Isaacson, W. (2008). *Einstein: His Life and Universe*. New York: Simon & Schuster.

Johnstone, T., & Walter, H. (2014). The Neural Basis of Emotion Dysregulation in Gross, James J. *Handbook of Emotion Regulation, Second Edition*. New York: Guilford Press.

Jones, C., Kirkland, T., & Cunningham. (2014). Attitudes, Evaluation, and Emotion Regulation in Gross, James J. *Handbook of Emotion Regulation, Second Edition*. New York: Guilford Press.

Kabat-Zinn, J. An Outpatient Program in Behavioral Medicine for Chronic Pain Patients Based on the Practice of Mindfulness Meditation: Theoretical Considerations and Preliminary Results. *General Hospital Psychiatry*, 4(1), 33 – 47.

Kabat-Zinn, John. (2005). *Wherever You Go, There You Are.* 10th Edition. New York: Hachette Books.

Kubzansky, L. D., Cole, S. R., Kawachi, I., Vokonas, P. S. & Sparrow, D. (2006). Shared and Unique Contributions of Anger, Anxiety, and Depression to Coronary Heart Disease: A Prospective Study in the Normative Age Study. *Annals of Behavioral Medicine*, 31, pp. 21–29.

Kubzansky, L. D., Park, N., Peterson, C., Vokonas, P., & Sparrrow, D. (2011). Healthy Psychological Functioning and Incident Coronary Heart Disease: The Importance of Self-Regulation. *Archives of General Psychiatry*, 68, pp. 400–408.

Kuhn, T. S. (1957). *The Copernican Revolution: Planetary Astronomy in the Development of Western Thought.* Cambridge: Harvard University Press.

Leary, M. R. & Tate, E. B. (2007). The Multi-Faceted Nature of Mindfulness. *Psychological Inquiry*, 18, pp. 251–255.

LeDoux, J. E. (2000). Emotion circuits in the brain. *Annual Review of Neuroscience*, 23(1), pp. 155-184.

MacPhillamy, D. J., & Lewinsohn, P. M. (1982). The Pleasant Events Sched- ule: Studies on Reliability, Validity, and Scale Intercorrelation. *Journal of Consulting and Clinical Psychology,* 50, pp. 363-380.

MacLeod, C., & Grafton, B. (2014). Regulation of Emotion through Modification of Attention, in Gross, James J. *Handbook of Emotion Regulation, Second Edition*. New York: Guilford Press.

McLeod, S. A. (2018, May 03). *Erik Erikson's stages of psychosocial development*. Retrieved from *https://www.simplypsychology.org/Erik-Erikson.html*

Mapscaping. Online, 2019.

Mass, I., & Tamir, M. (2014). Emotion Goals: How Their Content, Structure, and Operation Shape Emotion Regulation, in Gross, James J. *Handbook of Emotion Regulation, Second Edition*. New York: Guilford Press.

Marra, T. (2004). Depressed & Anxious: *The Dialectical Behavior Workbook*. Oakland, CA.: New Harbinger.

Marra, T. (2005). *Dialectical Behavior Therapy in Private Practice*. Oakland: New Harbinger.

Masicampo, E. J. & Bameister, R. F. Relating Mindfulness and Self-Regulatory Processes. *Psychological Inquiry*, 18, pp. 255–258.

McKay, M., Davis, M., & Fanning, P. (2011). *Thoughts & Feelings*. Oakland, CA.: New Harbinger.

McKay, M., Wood, J., & Brantley, J. (2007). *The Dialectical Behavior Therapy Skills Workbook*. Oakland, CA.: New Harbinger.

Mesquita, Batja, De Leersnyder, Jozefien, and Albert, Dustin. The Cultural Regulation of Emotions, in Gross, James J: Handbook of Emotion Regulation, Second Edition. Guilford Press: New York, 2014

Minden, Joal. How Much Does Homework Matter in Therapy? Psychology Today: Online, 2017.

Moore, A. and Malinowski, P. Meditation Mindfulness and Cognitive Flexibility. Consciousness and Cognition, 18, 176 – 186, 2009.

Morgan, W. D., and Morgan, S. T. Cultivating Attention and Empathy in C. K. Germer, R. D. Siegel, and P. R. Fulton Mindfulness and Psychotherapy, 73 – 90. New York: Guilford Press, 2005.

Ochsner, Kevin N and Gross, James J. The Neural Bases of Emotion and Emotion Regulation, in Gross, James J: Handbook of Emotion Regulation, Second Edition. Guilford Press: New York, 2014.

Oxford English Dictionary. Oxford University Press: Oxford, United Kingdom, 2001.

Proudfit, Greg Hajak, Dunning, Jonathan P., Foti, Daniel and Weinberg, Anna. Temporal Dynamics of Emotion Regulation, in Gross, James J: Handbook of Emotion Regulation, Second Edition. Guilford Press: New York, 2014.

Roberson, Cliff and Wallace, Paul H. Family Violence: Legal, Medical, and Social Perspectives. Routledge: New York, 2016.

Russell, J, A. Core Affect and the Psychological Construction of Emotion. Psychology Review. 110, 145 – 172, 2003.

Ryan, R. M. and Deci, E. L. On Happiness and Human Potentials: A Review of Research on Hedonic and Eudaimonic Well Being. Annual Review of Psychology. 52:141 -166, 2001.

Shapiro, S. L., Carlson, L. E., Astin, J. A., and Feldman, B. Mechanisms of Mindfulness. Journal of Clinical Psychology, 62, 373 – 386, 2006.

Sheppes, Gail. Emotion Regulation Choice: Theory and Findings, in Gross, James J: Handbook of Emotion Regulation, Second Edition. Guilford Press: New York, 2014.

Siegel, D. J. The Mindful Brain: Reflection and Attunement in the Cultivation of Well-Being. Norton: New York, 2007.

Thompson, Ross A. Socialization of Emotion and Emotion Regulation in the Family, in Gross, James J: Handbook of Emotion Regulation, Second Edition. Guilford Press: New York, 2014.

Tracy, Jessica. Pride: The Secret of Success. Houghton Mifflin Harcourt: Boston, 2016.

Tusinska, Magdalena. Buddhist Economics as a New Mindset at the Business Level, in Economic and Social Development Book of Proceedings. Varazin Development and Entrepreneurship Agency (VADEA), 148 – 157), May 23 – May 24, 2019.

Västfjäl, Daniel, Slovic, Paul, Burns, William, Erlandsson, Avid, Koppell, Linda, Asutay, Erkin, and Tinghog, Gustav. The Arithmetic of Emotion: Integration of Incidental and Integral Affect in Judgments and Decisions, Frontiers in Psychology, 7:325, 2016.

Wallace, B. A. Intersubjectivity in Indo-Tibetan Buddhism. Journal of Consciousness Studies, 8, 209 – 230, 2001.

Wallin, D. J. Attachment in Psychotherapy. New York: Guilford Press, 2007.

Walker, J., Sharpe, M.. & Wessley, S. Commentary: Symptoms Not Associated with Disease: An Unmet Public Health Challenge. International Journal of Epidemiology, 35, 477 – 478, 2006.

Walsh, R. and Shapiro, S. L. The Meeting of Meditative Disciplines and Western Psychology: A Mutually Enriching Dialogue. American Psychologist, 61, 227 – 239, 2006.

Weizmann Institute of Science. Quantum Theory Demonstrated: Observation Affects Reality (1998, February 27). Science Daily. Retrieved July 30, 2019 Online.

Williams, J. M. G. (2010). Mindfulness and Psychological Process. *Emotion*, 10, pp. 1–7.

Young, S. (1997). *The Science of Enlightenment*. Boulder: Sounds True.

Zimmerman, P., & Thompson, R. (2014). New Directions in Developmental Emotion Regulation Research Across the Life Span. *International Journal of Behavioral Development*.

Practice Worksheets

Photocopy these forms blank so you can use them repeatedly as a journal, monitor your progress, and prompt repetition of the skills.

Practice Mindfulness
With The Senses

Example: Date – **Wednesday**
Sound—Opened window and listened to the birds chirp for 5 min.
Taste—Mindfully ate my fish and ate spinach slowly, tasted each bite, paused between each forkful

Thursday
Tactile—Mindfully pet my dog 5 min.
Visual – Looked at flowers mindfully

Date		
Sound		
Smell		
Tactile		
Visual		
Taste		

Identify The Prompting Events for Your Feelings

Feelings	Situations That Make Me Feel That Way
Example: Disappointment	My husband has not told me all week that he loves me.

Evaluating New Threat Situations

Ask yourself if the treat is real or imagined/only feared

New Threat	Plan To Deal With The Threat
Example: If I hear one more criticism of me I will scream.	Dad has always been critical, guess he thinks it is his role as a father. I'll listen to him nonreactively and ask myself if his comments are good for me or not. I'll relax, deep breathe, and not necessarily reply.

Positive Feelings Journal

Increase the total number daily

Date	What I Did	How I Felt

New and Renewed Positive Experiences

Expanded Positive Experience (Never Did It Before)	What I Did	How It Made Me Feel
Rekindle— Remembering Through Prompts	What I Did	How It Made Me Feel
Re-membering (No Prompts)	What I Did	How It Made Me Feel
Vicarious Prompts (Watching Others)	What I Did	How It Made Me Feel
Self-Compassionate Statements	What I Said To Myself	How It Made Me Feel

Reframing Negative Situations

Painful/Annoying Situation	Reframe/Alternative Perspective

Body Relaxation

Date	Method Used (Deep Breathing, Progressive or Body Scan)	How I Felt

Acceptance and Tolerance

Date	What I Accepted or Tolerated	How I Felt

Roles, Values, and Bonding

Date	What Role I Played, What Value I Enacted, Or How I Bonded With Others	How It Made Me Feel
July 1	Purchased groceries for the dish I'm making for the 4th of July celebration	Made me aware of how important my friends and family are to me (bonding)

Narratives, Assertion, and Wise Behavior
What I Did Today

Date	New Narrative Behavior To Engage It	Assertive Behavior	How I Behaved Wisely
Nov 4	I can stand up to John and feel good about doing so. My self-worth is not based on what I can do for others (codependency)	Told John I would not write his essay, that he was capable of doing it himself.	I did not make a big deal about it—just said no and went about my business

Problems and How to Resolve Them

Problem/Symptom	Strategy To Resolve	Refer to Pages
Too emotional	Use Strategy, Problem Solving Maybe not too emotional	8, 12, 15 – 19
Do I need a therapist?	Since you ask, probably	10
I have more risks than I can handle	Re-evaluate your Threat Assessments	52 – 58
I feel too deeply	Such a thing? Focus on Body	12, 30 – 38
I don't feel deeply enough	Expand Positive Experiences Mindfulness	59 – 75, 30 – 38
I feel threatened	Re-asses Threat, Remove Yourself From Situation	52 – 58, 113 – 115, 124 – 125
I hate myself/disappointed in myself	Self-Compassion	81 – 86
Avoidance & Procrastination	Acceptance and Tolerance	93 – 101, 135 – 137
I feel overwhelmed	Focus on Body, Mindfulness	125 – 127, 21 – 37
No meaning in my life	Mindfulness, Meditation	14 – 15, 60 – 65
I feel disconnected from others	Consider Context, Culture, Bonding and Community Activities	149 – 158, 177 – 184, 196
My job sucks	Values	52, 177, 195, 16
People say I'm immature	Examine Stages of Development and see what life tasks you missed	192 – 194
I'm disconnected from my experience; I don't feel joy	Mindfulness	21 – 33
I hate my life	Re-Do Meaning	194 – 195
I keep making mistakes	Attention and Attribution	12 – 17, 81 – 87
No fun in my life	Expand Positive Experiences	217, 68 – 74
Too much pain in my life	Decentering, Remove Self From Situation, Body Focus, Tolerance	113 – 121, 135 – 138
My life is always out of balance	Long-Term vs. Short-Term	97 – 106, 7 – 8

I'm not getting anything out of twhis book	Probably you are reading the book as you would a novel, rather than working the book through doing the exercises. Seek a psychologist or Life Coach,	8 - 10
People tell me I've got it all wrong	Attributions, Misattributions	15 - 17
Nobody loves me	Self-Compassion	81 - 87
People tell me I'm too big for my britches	Comparisons	82 - 83
I'm frustrated nobody ever listens	Reappraisal, Family Context	104- 105, 150 - 153
Why can't I get what I want sometimes?	Attributions, Assertion	183, 15 – 17, 172 - 177
Other people are strange	Comparisons	82 - 85
What anger? I'm not angry!	Denial	90 - 93
You always think you are better than me	Comparisons	82 - 85
Opinions are cheap	Values	102 – 106, 152 - 158
Whatever happened to fair play?	Comparisons, Assertion	82 – 85, 172 – 175
YOU are the problem	Comparisons	82 – 85, 90 - 93
I'm lost. I don't know where to turn	Emotional Problem Solving	8
There are too many "should" coming from others. What about what I want?	Re-read Denial, Assertion	90 – 93, 172 - 175
I love my family, but they hurt me so much	Re-read Context and Self	176 – 182
The world is full of evil	Attributions	15 – 17, 17, 41 – 47, 60 - 63
Why me? I always seem to get the short end of the stick	Comparisons, Winning, Assertion	143 – 144, 172 - 177
Seems like everyone is blowing things out of perspective	Denial	90 - 93
I just want to be happy	Increase Positive Emotional Experiences	68 - 74

I just want others to be happy	Assertion, Narrative	172 – 175, 163 - 171
I'm doing as much as I can. Seems like it is never enough	Maps, Assertion	139 – 148, 172 - 175
I just want to sleep this bad dream called life away. Wake me when it is over	Increase Positive Emotional Experiences	68 – 74, 106 - 110
I'm paralyzed, emotionally. I don't know what to do that would be helpful.	Avoidance Increase Positive Emotional Experiences	16 – 18, 68 – 74, 8 - 10
No matter how much I give to others, it is not enough. They want more	Comparisons, Context, Maps, Assertiveness	82 – 83, 149 - 162
I'm anxious and afraid	Mindfulness, Relaxation	218, 125 - 135
I don't know what to do	Emotional Problem Solving	8 - 9
Why can't I just give up?	Rumination, Avoidance	13 – 15, 109 – 111, 93 - 101
Why does everyone else have it so easy?	Comparisons, Narrative	81 – 83, 163 - 171
I'm a good person. Why do so many bad things come my way?	Comparisons, Narrative	81 – 83, 163 - 171
Why don't others recognize how special and loving I am?	Maps, Semantics, Comparisons, Narrative	184, 141 – 142, 160 - 171